This book was a wonderful journey and has only been made possible from the help and closeness of so many people I want to thank. Thanks to Tina Ciccarelli and her Association for welcoming me to Padua.

Thanks to all my friends from Padua, primarily Davide and Gianni, for the affection and the support they have given me during these years.

Thank you to all my old friends, who every time I go back to my origins, they never let me miss their friendship.

Thanks to Francesca Casarotto, my lawyer. Thanks to Ornella.

Thanks to my family, my amazing sisters Maria and Lucia.

Thank you to my brothers-in-law Toni and Vincenzo and all my aunts, uncles and cousins.

Thanks to my brother Gianni, the other half of me: this book is for him. I dedicate these pages and my own life to him.

Finally, I thank my parents, Salvatore and Antonina, to whom I owe the beginning of my life and the man I am.

- S.R.

The coherence of your ideas

and your choices

it is an added value that has a price.

I paid him

and I'll always pay for it,

in solitude and suffering.

But with the knowledge that I'm proud.

Foreword

I liked Salvo from the moment I started working with him, & over the years the respect has continued to grow deeper & deeper. Not only does he have a great sense of humor, but he is also well educated, naturally sharp, driven, & grounded to the rhythms of business, too. It takes a lot of patience to allow the cogs of process to turn, often slowed down due to "the surname known throughout the world", but Salvo knows this all too well - his life has not been an easy one.

This book was written some years before its release in English, and as such is written in the then present tense. Much has happened since; & my guess is if you are reading this then you will probably be aware of such losses in the life of the Riina family. This book is an insight into their family life that is simply not possible to see anywhere else.

It is a privilege to be Salvo's personal representative/manager in the English speaking 'West'- a role I take extremely seriously, & along with our wider Company (PYLE & FRANCIS) with my business partner Joey Pyle Jnr, we are acting as promoters as well as agents for his current & future ventures in the United Kingdom, United States of America, Republic of Ireland, Canada, Australia, New Zealand to name but a few. Ventures that include further written works, business, Film/TV, interviews, events, & much more.

With new blood, comes a new day.

Will Francis

(PYLE & FRANCIS)

Table of Contents

Chapter 1: La telefonata

Chapter 2: Di casa in casa

Chapter 3: L'amore di un latitante

Chapter 4: Il figlio di Bellomo

Chapter 5: Motivi di opportunità

Chapter 6: 23 maggio 1992

Chapter 7: La strada brucia

Chapter 8: Arrivederci Palermo

Chapter 9: Una nuova famiglia

Chapter 10: Il pianto di un padre

Chapter 11: Un bacio e una carezza

Chapter 12: I fratelli Riina

Chapter 13: Una visita indiscreta

Chapter 14: Senza Giovanni

Chapter 15: Un ricordo di sangue

Chapter 16: Tentativi di futuro

Chapter 17: Gli occhi della polizia

Chapter 18: Totòs

Chapter 19: Terremoto alle 2:37

Chapter 20: Il canile della Sicilia

Chapter 21: Le montagne profumano

Chapter 22: Addio, appuntato

Chapter 23: Lucia si sposa

Chapter 24: Un ergastolo in bianco

Chapter 25: Diritti e doveri

Preface

Salvo Riina is the third child of Totò Riina and Ninetta Bagarella. Giovanni, the another son, is serving a life sentence like his father Totò. Salvo Riina, a year younger than Giovanni, has recently finished serving an 8-years and 10 months sentence for Mafia association. He now lives in Padua, Italy, where he is on probation for the next two years. His father, Totò Riina, is referred to by everyone as "il capo dei capi" of Cosa Nostra and is served life imprisonment, having been found guilty of heinous murders.

Salvo Riina, however, felt the need to write this book, not to challenge the various convictions of the judges, but to describe life from within his family. To show the dynamics that develop in a family where their children, just teenagers, know that their father is called Giuseppe Bellomo and by profession he is a surveyor, who cannot attend any kind of school, who changed their homes several times a year, and who everyone respects this strange surveyor, wherever they go to live. And this remained until January 1993, when Totò Riina was captured.

They go to live in Corleone, of which they had so much heard of, but they had never set foot in it. Thus, begins the realization of who actually was their father, they begin to make themselves account of how hard life is being followed step by step from law enforcement and how hard it is, if not impossible, to look for your own way with that last name that they find themselves. However, there is also a growing awareness that, in any case, Totò Riina was the father they played with, lived with and who loved them.

The result is a completely different glimpse of family life from the ordinary, which shows us not "il capo dei capi", but a man with his weaknesses, with his own Feelings.

The attitude of the mother also stands out, Ninetta Bagarella, who played the role of "teacher at home" for the preparation of their own children, having not had the opportunity to attend normal schools having been born "a fugitive". And that's why the relationship of the four children with mom has been, and is, very tight.

A biography that is an absolute novelty in this genre and that, knowing how to read in watermark, communicates moments and situations that we would never have thought could develop into such a particular family.

In the end it is the attempt to open a dialogue with the many readers who will read these pages. Perhaps this is the real reason why Salvo Riina has wanted to write this book. After so much silence it is finally time to show what was the family life of Totò Riina.

Chapter 1: La Telefonata
The Phone Call

"Ten minutes."
A voice comes behind me.
"The phone call. Or have you not thought about it?"
I slowly open my eyes and listen. It is the voice of the guard, there is no doubt, because, when a policeman talks to you, you recognize him immediately by the masterful tone. I get slowly up and I recognize him with his snake eye. I remember him; I remember him. Yesterday he made a fuss when I asked him for more soap to wash my shirt. I grab it and I don't say anything.
"So Riina, what are we going to do? Are we going to get up or do you expect breakfast?""
"I wasn't asleep. I was resting my eyes," I reply, and complete the rise by sinking the hands in the mattress.

For a moment I must have fallen asleep, and dreamed of being away from here. In a less dirty place but above all with more light. In April, they told me who would send me away from Padua for a moment I hesitated: Voghera, I did not know even where it was. Here the sun is not ever enough.... it is not enough for those who live here as a free citizen, let alone for us detainees. The second one opens the cell door to me and, without adding anything else, beckons me to go out. When there are visiting days, I am always restless even if they're just Telephone calls. Of course, I don't expect anyone to come up here to Pavia to see me, and I have no other way of talking to my father if not through a call. We've been doing this for years, this life in my family, in a network of travel and letters, from north to south, just to feel a little less alone.

My name is Giuseppe Salvatore Riina, or Salvo to my friends, detained in the prison of Voghera since April 2011. My journey had begun much earlier, nine years ago, with my arrest in Corleone. Like me, they detained my brother Giovanni, in Spoleto, and my father Salvatore, for all Totò. Toto Riina. Since I was a child, I have been used to seeing my father every day, no day excluded. Now I have to ask permission through a piece of paper to be able to just talk. I'm starting to walk down the hall of my section, the phone is right at the bottom, and the guard who came to pick me up tramples me in the shadow, following me, careful to follow every movement of mine, even if I were able to disappear at any moment.

Living in our conditions means not being able to choose anything from one's life, times, needs and desires. What we can choose sometimes seems more of a joke than a concession: for example, we can decide whether to see a family member of ours privately, or simply talk to him on the phone. Once a month, only one. Ten minutes of phone call to make from prison to prison even if you're a free citizen: the shame of entering a prison you still have to suffer it. Ten minutes on the phone or an hour of in-person visit. Today is August 7, 2011, and I asked to talk to my father. This month I will be his only window into the world; My mother will have to give up seeing her husband and Giovanni to hear his father. Like genies of the lamp, we have only one wish at the month to be expressed, and therefore also the love of the family must be dosed and distributed equally among all those who suffer.

"Wait here until it sounds."
"I know how it works," I reply to the Guard.

The phone rings, the switchboard tells me not to wait any longer. I try to relax by looking around, but there's nothing that's any help. A room the size of a closet, a wooden chair squeaking, above the coffee table a phone that seems to have come out of a Sip advertisement from the 1990s. The guard walked away, leaving me alone and now he checks me at a distance of about ten meters. You don't even have to wonder in those who will listen to this phone call, between policemen and magistrates, who with pen and paper in their hands and who with the recorder. But in the family now we are used to seeing every move we make turned into a legend and every word in the process. Finally, here's the free line. I'm going to take a long breath and I try to feel properly alone with my father.

'Hello, Salvo?'
'Dad?'
'Salvo, yes?'
"I'm fine. And you, how are you?"

Every time, the same questions. I feel his voice and a warmth clutches my chest. I guess so, as I am now, within this closet full of eyes and ears, sitting on the chair clutching the receiver with both hands, as if in a hug.

"Better, I'm getting rest."
'Controls?' "They made them for me, don't worry. What about you? When do you get out?'
"I'm going out in October, maybe. I don't believe it much."
"What about Mom?" he asks me.

I think about how he will have to go another month before he can hear our voices. I must try to live up to this phone call.

"Of course, she's happy." Another silence. Ten minutes pass quickly.

"Giovanni too he's fine." I say

'Have you decided where to go?'.

"Yes, Dad. I want to go back to Padua."

"But why, what's in Padua?" he asks me worried. He must have the impression that I do not want to return to Corleone for a while.

"But yes. You know that. Be careful."

"I know, it's not easy anywhere."

If a stranger spoke in this moment on the phone with my father, they would have many more questions to ask him than I have now. Yet this shyness there's never been until we have been separated by the bars of a prison. When I get out of here, I will go to Padua to serve my months of special surveillance because in Sicily now there is nothing left that can do me good, and the looks of the people weigh ten times as much. In Sicily it takes little to get a finger pointing at you, or to make the cops suspicious. But I will stay in the north, to finish serving in peace all the guilt that Italian justice will still want to recognize from me.

"But stay close to mom."

"Don't worry."

"And to Lucia", he specifies.

My father and sister have always had an extraordinary relationship, but too short. When he was arrested, she was twelve years old, and still had to see so many of these things. The conversation lasts a few more words before a prolonged whistle in the phone to indicate that the ten minutes are over.

"I embrace you, Salvo. Goodnight. Listen well."

"Bye, Dad."

I breathe deep again. I would like to vent, but the guard is already at my shoulders and the script repeats itself, equal and humiliating, as always. I waited seven months to hear that voice and I already have to work off memories. This is my father to me. Words that have a value, a hug, a weight and a certainty. This is my Totò Riina, and this is my family.

Chapter 2. Di casa in casa
From house to house

I was born on May 3, 1977 in Palermo. The clinic, one of the best in town, hosted us more days than expected, being forced to over a week in an incubator due to some complications. My father came at all hours, leaned to the glass and looked at me anxiously for my health.

"Salvo, aiutati che Dio ti aiuta"
"Salvo, God helps those that help themselves," he repeated all the time. And God helped me. He has always been a fatalist, my father, from when I was born to when I became a man. He followed the life of his family with love and believing that fate would take its course when a normal person would have fear of difficulties.

I was born in the clinic, like my brothers, and as they were, I recorded with my real name: Giuseppe Salvatore Riina. There was no fear of being recognized, in those years, perhaps because the times were different, and you spoke less of certain things. It felt safe and so we all were registered at the registry. My sister Maria Concetta on December 19th 1974, my brother Giovanni Francesco on 21 February 1976 and Lucia, the youngest, on 11th November 1980. In just six years the house was filled with screams and laughter. Of course, the house wasn't always the same, because something unusual was happening for us Children. Unusual and at the same time fun. We moved often, to the city or to countryside, and our rooms changed number and size. It wasn't a pain, but a game, in fact.

Since 1969 my father was a fugitive and with the time we were too, his family from whom he never separated, we became a little migratory. My brothers and I understood that a new journey was on the horizon from the glances of our parents. There was always a certain trepidation. My father consulted with my mother, who always accepted everything with love and devotion, and the first bags appeared out of the door of the closet or the attic. Maria Concetta and Giovanni were of little age difference to me, but they understood at once the situation and, imitating mom and dad, confabulated in a whisper.

"You don't talk in your ear!" I cried, and out of spite they insisted on making me believe that there was some secret of which I didn't have to be made aware.

"We leave tomorrow, but we are leaving you here. Mom told us,"

As they took me around, I was beginning to cry because there's no worse nightmare for a child than that of being abandoned by the family. I ran to my dad to vent and ask if the threat were true; he smiled at me with those deep eyes of his, so similar to mine, and caressed my head as to say, "I'm not leaving you anywhere."

I've never been a child of those capricious or spoiled types, much less one with the easy tear, but Mary and Giovanni sometimes they were doing everything they could to make me angry. Always allied against me in games or hide-and-seek, blind fly, or games from the table. When they closed me in a room, for example, and I was shouting so much that even the neighbors heard me. We played, like all normal families, even when we started to understand that we were little more of a special family than others.

The day arrived before each new departure, our mother appeared at the threshold of the bedroom and stared at us. At last, she would defend me, I hoped.

   We're leaving in the morning."
   "For where?" asked Maria without batting an eyelash.
   "A new home."
   'In Palermo?'
   "Let's hope it's that cottage in the country " I said.

There I had a whole room just for me and the earth smelled of a pleasant fragrance. I kept quiet, waiting as it was "the greats" who spoke. My mother, like my father, answered with a smile and took the suitcase for our things. There was an all-orange one that we only filled with toys, and I never lost sight of it. One day, I can't say exactly when, I realized that we were changing homes every time someone had found out where we were. But I understood it myself for whatever reason it was not an important topic to discuss at the table. For my father everything was right so, and he did not feel guilty because we did not give him a way. At the table, rather, there was talk of sport, of movies, games and studio. Us Riina brothers were not allowed to go to school, it would have been too risky, and therefore even our education was singular: my mother took care of it, every day, morning and afternoon, and we were not given to garnish... not a bit.

   "Did you finish your homework?" my father asked.
   "You have to study, study makes people the best!"
He would add, *"Testa cu'n parra si chiama cucuzza!"* An old Sicilian proverb meaning "It is much better to talk, at the cost of making mistakes, than to sound like a pumpkin." and we all would go down laughing. He had the third grade, and for that

reason he did not compromise on certain aspects. For my father the people who counted, those who we saw on television, even politicians, they had come up because they had studied and they had made a position. And so his children, one day, would become important ones like them.

Chapter 3: L'amore di un Latitante
Love of a Fugitive

If my father was often out during the day, the constant certainty was our mother. Antonina Bagarella had never pulled back in front of anything, a modern woman and strong one at that, while knowing the difficulties of the life that she had chosen, was and still is a pillar for the whole family.

The earliest memories I have of my mother are those of a beautiful girl, with dark eyes and the very black and long hair that descends on her shoulders. There was a picture that my father stared often in love and that we carried following in every journey: he barely depicted her of three-quarters, with a clear complexion and the gaze fixed forward. It was she who wanted to call me Giuseppe, after one of her brothers, sent to confinement many years before, and as happened also included the name of my grandfather.

Another of my uncles, on the other hand, had remained in Corleone, a childhood friend and great confidant of Dad. Uncle Calogero and my father were always together, and day after day Ninetta's eyes fell in love more and more of this cheerful village and busy man. It was 1955 when they first saw each other. At the time Toto was fourteen years older than her, and never hid his troubled life. When she was still beginning to walk, he, at eighteen, already suffered the first arrest. When she was in her twenties, she was studying at the university of Palermo, he was already known for the Bari trial of 1964. My mother always wanted to choose all of her life, even when the encounters with the man she loved began to be cadenced by my father's escapes in and around Sicily.

My grandmother, Lucia Mondello, had improvised as a seamstress since my grandfather Salvatore had ended up in confinement, and wished that his daughters always remained close to him. But my mother had already graduated from high school. Classic, in a class with only five women, and now she was aiming for a degree.

"Girls should stay in the house! They don't go around studying, far from the family!", thundered grandma and my uncle Leoluca on everyone.

"It is not dignified for a woman to travel alone to Palermo!"

Ninetta had enrolled in university and in the meantime taught physical education at the institute Corleone, an institute of nuns who instead admired the passion of the young teacher. She was the most modern of the family and would defend at every cost her choices. So, she also defended her love.

In the parish festivals of Santa Rosalia, always looking into Totò's eyes, because he was the guy she most admired and wanted for herself. She was impressed by his honesty, from his being a real man, with values of other times. He was invited to dance, but only because she chose him, and my father loved her resourcefulness and energy. If they had not been what they still are, they could never stand the life that awaited them. At the trial of Bari, my father was acquitted but was still forced to special surveillance in San Giovanni in Persiceto, in the province of Bologna, and so in 1969 it all began.

Fugitive is a state of life that takes you away from friendships, sincere ones, and makes you alone. If you're not able to be enough for yourself, you can't do it. Every month, every discovery, you have to be ready to go and start again: sometimes some friend lends you the house, or rents, paying a substantial advance for avoiding hassle. Even when we were born, we children lived under these conditions. But from the dances, from those looks, from that we huddle happily as the orchestra in the square played Canzonette, a love was born. Among many friendships with the Bagarella family, the most precious gift to my father was the love of his long dark haired, Ninetta. Following a man who did not have a home was a choice to make with love and fidelity. So, my mother accepted the years of surveillance imposed on her as the first price of shared fugitiveness. She was to be sent to confinement, but her arguments would have convinced any judge. "I'm a girl just in love with her man," she said. As my father continued his travels, in 1971 she was forced to two years of fixed dwelling in Corleone. Three times a week she had to go to the police station to sign, and never could get out of the house before eight o'clock in the morning or after eight o'clock in the evening. There were those who felt ashamed for her, but my mother, despite suffering these limitations, was proud of her choices and so she accepted the twelve hours a day that were granted to go out the door. A woman who had lived all her life in Corleone, who knew the stones, the trees, the names and surnames of the people in the radius of a mile, now counted the days that separated her from seeing her boyfriend.

Nostalgia time ended April 16th 1974, in a discreet chapel in the countryside Palermo. A priest friend of the family and few relatives found themselves finally at Salvatore Riina's and Antonina Bagarella's wedding.

"We cannot go to the Municipality for the recording," my father explained.
"It does not matter, we need the blessing of God and Santa Rosalia" she smiled
"You know that I am older than you, and that we're going to have to hide."
"It doesn't matter. We will be a family and we're not going to need anything more."
"Where do you want to go for your honeymoon?"

"Venice," replied my mother.

Since the playing of a song by Claudio Villa in the square in order to tighten the life of that young, beautiful girl, to when they could make their first trip together, nineteen years of engagement had passed. My mother was in her thirties. and my father forty-four. Whenever they could, even in front of the eyes of us children, shameful and shy, my parents never stopped wanting to exchange caresses. Sometimes a song on tv or radio made them go back in time; then they took each other by the hand and they told us about this country, Corleone, the girls, and the parties. I had heard so many times about Corleone, but who knows why we never went there.

Chapter 4: Il figlio di Bellomo
Bellomo's Son

"Have you studied the chapter on Manzoni?"
"Of course I studied it. I won't tell you again."
"I only remember that of the promised married is called as Grandmother Lucia."
"That's Mondella, not Mondello! You're terrible at this!" I laughed with my brother Giovanni as we finished getting dressed in the morning. Grandma also lived in Corleone and I had never met her. My mother often spoke of there.

"If you make me a copy of the math exercise, I promise today I won't lock you in the room."
"I'm not going to make you a copy of anything at all. You know mom notices when it is not you," I concluded.

I head for the kitchen. The table was already ready: books, sheets of paper, a case in the center with pens of all colors and the metal blackboard dangling from a cupboard knob.

"What should I notice?" she asked with folded arms, waiting for the class to fill up.

Not even to say it, it was just me and Giovanni, for Maria was already sitting with the notebook in front of her to review. Our idea of school, until adolescence, was different from that of all the other children our age but not for this less fun. For two hours in the morning, and as many in the afternoon, the kitchen became our classroom. Mom, with a professor's take that she had never lost, she was our teacher in everything: Italian, history, geography, mathematics, physics. She was not just capable but an intelligent woman and always prepared. Every morning she explained to us history and Italian, using one of the many books that we carried with us every move. We changed houses but the kitchen remained always the perfect place delegated to teaching. Of course, because, between a sentence and the other, between a question to Giovanni and one to me, could keep the stove under control. It was satisfying to know that, thanks to our lessons, the sauces never stick to the pots and roasts did not burn ever!

With one move, Ninetta was a teacher, mother and housewife. Even my father, when he wasn't out of the house for work, overlooked the kitchen. He was one of those rare men who liked to cook, and when he did he could do so very well. On those occasions Mom, quieter, would distract herself from the cooking and explain the more complicated things, such as the exercises in mathematics or physics. I had fun stretching my neck to see that behind her, facing the base of the sink, there he was struggling with vegetables from shredding or with a sauté going on. Every so often we exchanged eyes of complicity, he would wink at me and I, happy, would come back to follow my mother's words. When I could, I ran to help him, and proudly I announced, "Today the men cook at home!" Maria Concetta was the best as a student, and not only because she was the oldest; I was going strong in geography while Giovanni... well, he was headstrong and so was not looking forward to finishing up, but rather playing again.

We have inhabited condominiums with three rooms and a bathroom, while other times the houses were luxurious and full of spaces. There was always a room that we used as a room of the games and we spent hours there having fun and, of course, to quarrel. Until the afternoon, when another two hours of class awaited us dedicated to exercises and review. None of our houses were too rich or flashy. This moderate lifestyle and discreetness was what my father wanted. Just so as not to give too much in the eye. *"U picca abbasta e l'assai assuviecchia"* He always said. "That which is small, is enough and that which is too much overflows." He hated flaunting well-being, and he ensured that we too knew how to behave with the other people we met.

One of the first tests I was subjected to was in the spring of 1986. I was nine years old and at that time we were living in a nice apartment in the center of Palermo: one of the most elegant houses I can remember. As in all other places we had no type of phone inside the house, therefore, if we wanted to talk to friends and have fun, there was no other solution than to go out to play in the middle of the road. I had little company, one of the many things I have changed in those years, and among these children there was one bigger than the others. I do not remember the name of the girl, except that she was fourteen years old. In spite of my shyness, I preferred to look at those bigger than me, and she was not only taller, but also more beautiful and certainly more attractive than my ten-year-old peers. I wanted to give my first kiss to her, so one day I escorted her back at home and, when we were alone, I asked her very frankly.

"Why should I give you a kiss?" She asked.
"I don't know. Because I want it."
"You're a child. I don't kiss them so young."
"But tomorrow I leave," I invented.

After all, it was a very likely lie.
"Who knows when we meet again."
"I don't even know who you are. So, all I know is where you live... but you never tell us anything about you.

"Do you know where I live?"

"Are you not in the house at the bottom of the road?"

"Yes, I live there."

"It's a beautiful palace. But what work does your father do?"

Often friends would ask me this question. I had rehearsed in front of the mirror to repeat what my parents had taught me. After all, I thought, that too was a game and it needed no explanation.

"My father? He is a surveyor for a company" was the answer I gave to anyone.

"The surveyor? And do you have that house over there? That beautiful?"

"How many questions you ask. But in short, now you want to give me this kiss? Yes or no?"

At the age of ten I had my first kiss to a girl five years older than me. A few days later, as I had predicted, we changed house again. I continued to be the son of Giuseppe Bellomo, a surveyor from Mazara del Vallo.

Chapter 5: Motivi di opportunità
Reasons for opportunity

My family never needed friends from outside to feel happier or more important. At the table in the evening, we were always six. Every day. Dad, Mom, Maria, Giovanni, and Lucia - we were enough and we constituted a clear example of happiness that I always remember with sweetness. There were never guests, and there was no day that we were not all together, in the everyday life as in the holidays. Even Christmas, for example, was the same of all the other families I knew, maybe even nicer. Wherever we were there was always a way to make tree and crib. The gifts were beautiful; tracks of the toy cars, board games, Meccano, and Lego. One or at most two gifts each, not to flaunt too much and not to spoil us: these were the house rules.

In the cold as in the heat, we moved always all together. I had no idea what exactly a fugitive was, but it had to be something nice if you were having so much fun. My father was not one like the other dads, this was clear to me. He didn't get up at dawn to go to the office and not even came back at sunset from the fields: he did another job that I did not know, however, such as most kids my age they often confuse the professions of parents. I knew that nothing was missing at home, and this seemed sufficient to me. In the summer we all left in the car to spend our beach holidays. Always in Sicily, of course, because there were no beaches more beautiful, and clean, than those of Agrigento, or of Trapani, or of Palermo. Sand and rocks, the umbrellas planted to defend children from the heat, stocks of water bottles and an African landscape. My dad sometimes went down to the beach with us and we played together to make castles of sand or shots on goal against Gianni. Other times, however, he did not want to cross the looks of others, so he stayed on the terrace of the villa, overlooking the sea to control us, with a newspaper in his hands to fathom who knows what news. If not the Sicilian coasts, then the farms near Bagheria or the countryside of Marineo would host us.

No one knew who we were, yet at the same time it seemed that everyone knew. On the street, in smaller centers, attention was aimed towards my father and us when we walked next to him. Never expressions of resentment, but always of respect and admiration. My father had a strong character and charisma, and I, holding him by the hand, felt confident that no one could hurt us. Unfortunately, however, we never all went out together, who knows why. Either with dad or with mom, but the Riina family was not granted a public walk, not even to go to Mass on Sundays. What would have Aunt Josepha said? A perpetual teacher of catechism. If she could have, at every mass skipped we would have given a cane on the hands, as she did with her school students.

"Why can't we all go out together? What if we do it for a time?"

"Reasons for expediency.", I was told in a laconic tone.

And over time things worsened. Towards the 90s the walks became increasingly rare. When I saw certain gestures of reverence and approval to my father, I looked at it from the bottom up and wondered the meaning of so much respect. Once I grew up, I wondered if that not it was fear, rather. There is no fear without respect, and what represented him to many of those people it was an example of justice and honesty. The same qualities that had already impressed my mother at the time of Corleone. Although the external outings decreased, I always found time to be with my father. We were two great sports fans and every discipline in which there was to compete – especially in team – to achieve an important result, we were excited. Between February and March 1992, we passed sleepless whole nights in front of the TV to follow the Moor of Venice compete in the America's Cup. Dad prepared the station of the sofa just for the two of us, with a cookie tray prepared for the occasion and two chairs placed like footrests. They were the best moments of the day, those where I could enjoy my father alone without the screams of Giovanni or the sisters, and the world remained in the dark: they remained outside the words of the news, those of politicians, those of the people who were on the street.

I had not yet turned fifteen years and he, Totò Riina, was my hero, who with his third grade he knew everything anyways that was important to know and that had nothing to do with what I had slowly begun to perceive from television.

Lucia, the little girl of the house, and I were the most beloved – woe to those who touched us! – and I was jealous of the minutes he spent just for me. We narrowly lost the America's Cup, but we viewers came out of it winners anyway: in the silence of home, illuminated only from the glow of the TV, turned on with a volume wire, sitting side by side, again I didn't realize I was spending one of the happiest moments of my life. Every morning my father would leave the house. He had a subcompact, old, which he crossed country after country, busy in business that he never told us. If it was something serious that happened and it was necessary a decision, the only confidant remained Ninetta, because we children did not need to understand.

There was no set time for his return but, as soon as you arrive at eight o'clock in the evening, someone still had the task of setting the table for six. Until the fateful January 1993, from what I remember, there was not a single day of our life in which my father slept outside the house. Anything could have happened, but before the dinner bell rang, he would be behind the door. Before eating, if there was time, or right away after that, he would put himself in his favorite armchair with newspapers in hand. His personal press review included a bunch of at least ten newspapers, from local newspapers to the national ones, commented in silence but always with greater expressive emphasis. It was the sign that there was something in the air new and terrible coming soon.

Chapter 6: 23 Maggio 1992
23 May 1992

That May 23rd was a Saturday. For starters, I remember it well because many of our friends they hadn't gone to school so we were able to spend the whole day with them and our scooters. I had just turned fifteen years old and every afternoon Giovanni and I got together with the rest of the group to chat or play a game of soccer. At that time we had a house in Palermo, and for teenagers like us it was a fortune, because in the city there was always the way to have fun and get distracted. We were growing up. The games in the countryside were beginning to stay there as we got tight.

The first memory I have of that Saturday is a reminder of sounds. A distant but fast echo reached our conversation. It was a siren. One was joined by two, then three, and again and again. Being in Palermo we were used to the sounds of traffic, emergencies, ambulance and police races, but slowly our eyes wondered more than words, because the background began to become constant. We left our stations, saddled of the mopeds, and we approached the bar.

"Have you heard?" The bartender asked Giovanni, He was motionless, with an empty glass in his hands, listening hypnotized to the radio.
"What happened?"
"I don't understand."
"There's police everywhere."
"They go to Capaci", added a little boy of our age, from behind the car of the espresso machine.
"They say they shot with a missile launcher in the tunnel."

We looked at each other. Suddenly the sound of sirens replaced everything. We said goodbye without adding anything. I had never seen Palermo in that way. There were people with spirited eyes, afraid, in a mixture of despair and surrender. I knew a missile launcher was not credible in Capaci, but in those late hours afternoon, when the Sun was still high in Sicily, each one interpreted as best could the news that came. There seemed to be a war on every street corner, and with Giovanni we had to slalom so many roads, too many, to gain the way back home. I still didn't know what to expect, but I was no longer a kid, and certain things I was beginning to recognize. Everyone was at home. We walked in and my mother immediately stared at us, without saying anything. The tv was turned on Tg1, and the news in edition extraordinary already went on for an hour. We didn't ask questions, but just limited ourselves to looking at the screen.

There was the face of Giovanni Falcone, that 23 May 1992, which was repeated every minute, alternating with revolting images of an open highway in two. We had made that tour many times to go to Trapani, and I remember the landscape of sea and mountains that you enjoy from that perspective. Now it was a steaming crater, full of debris and cops busy in the search. Me and my brother we were still standing watching in silence. My father Totò was also at home. He was sitting in his armchair in front of the television. He too in silence. He didn't say a word, but he was not agitated or particularly intrigued by those images. On his face a few wrinkles, just frowning, he listened thinking of something else and none of us had desire to discuss what happened. Tg1 became the background until the hour of dinner. It was nineteen thirty, and I locked myself in the room to think. Who was Falcone?... we all knew it in Palermo, and from that day things would change forever. The journalist was talking about claims and he spoke of "mafia", of clients, and the day after the pages of the newspapers were even more explicit: the name of the Riina was everywhere. Luckily my father flaunted serenity, and the burden on my family seemed more bearable.

Palermo became a militarized city, in which police, carabinieri and army they were lusted with exaggerated care. The funeral of Giovanni Falcone, his wife and the escort, I looked at them closed in at home, always on television, while my friends poured in the cathedral square to cry and shout, first of all against the State.

"I forgive you, but you must put yourself to kneel" cried one of the widows in live tv.

I listened and, like all words that I read in those weeks, I kept them to myself. Also, we talked less with Maria Concetta, and that spring it passed in a surreal way.

"Except, what did you do?" he always asked me my father when he saw me silent.
"Nothing, Dad," I replied.
"You, Salvo, you must be good."

When I was a kid, I always got asked why he addressed these words to me and not to Giovanni, who was the bigger male. Knowing that one day I would have been his support charged me of responsibility that I did not want, but to the at the same time I was proud.

"But no, Dad. You will always be fine. Not you will need me."
"Listen to me," he repeated.
" I will pass the baton to you in my old age."

The awareness of that situation of tension and control that was born on May 23 1992, prevented me from asking any questions to my father, and like me all the others of the family. I convinced myself that I was no longer a child and I accepted the perception that all of Italy in this moment was looking for Totò Riina, the leader of the chiefs, someone said. But life continued and we had to move forward, maybe even with consciousness. They would never take us.

Chapter 7: La Strada Brucia
The road burns

July is the best month to go to the sea in Sicily. The water is cleaner, the sun less scorching and especially the bathers are almost all Sicilians and not tourists coming from who knows where. My brothers and I went down on the beach armed with balloon, frisbee, masks and fins, while our mother is charged with a tower of towels with the thought that we could catch cold out of the water.

That July 19, 1992 was one of those days when my father preferred to stay in the house waiting for us, always surrounded by his newspapers that he read slowly but notedly. In recent months it had become more attentive in public outings, even if inside the house he was always the usual man smiling and willing to play.

When we got home it was late afternoon. Called by the screams of my mother who saw us running all over the shore, chasing a ball. Still dirty with sand and with the wet clothes we entered the living room where the tv was strangely already on. There was Tg1 and it was just eight o'clock: immediately the memories came back from a few months ago. In those days there were no satellite TVs and newscasts on every channel and at every moment, so when a broadcast or a movie was suddenly interrupted by the extraordinary edition theme song, we all stopped everyone worried while listening.

This time there was no image of a highway, but of a palace. A hole and many cars torn apart and smoking they occupied the entire roadway of Via D'Amelio. The journalist tried to creep in with the camera between the kicks, but the cops covered and censored the worse pictures. I found out later that it was to hide from the viewers' view of the mutilated bodies of the victims of the new attack. The magistrate Paolo Borsellino appeared in a box next to it, taken in a photo a few weeks before. This time I did not get the noises of ambulances as they ran outside but, after not even two months from what had happened to Capaci, the sound I could remember perfectly. Lucia, still twelve years old, was the most affected from those images. She approached my silent father.

"Dad, do we have to start again?"
"Why do you want to leave?" he asked, finally breaking the tension with which he was staring at the TV.
"I don't know. Do we have to go back to Palermo?
"You think about enjoying the holidays. Stay to the sea for a while longer."

Lucia burst into a naïve laugh and then hugged him, happy not to have to give up the summer entertainment and new friends made. And so, we stayed there until the end of August.

After the episode of Capaci, Palermo was transformed. After that of via D'Amelio, it had become unrecognizable. The air was changed, the military was everywhere and our life was difficult. There was a guy of our company who loved to talk of legality and mafia, but for the most part of us certain speeches seemed little unimpressive. Me, Giovanni and all the other friends of Palermo, we were unconscious and distracted, indifferent changes, as in the case of well-known "white sheets" hanging from the balconies. It began to become necessary to divert more often the roads we did on a scooter, because we couldn't take the risk to be stopped by the police. Our trips out of town were made of provincial roads and secondary, never of highways. In our pocket we lacked any kind of document. Riina was a name we couldn't reveal to no one, not even to the most trusted comrades. We were always the surveyor's children, and I often felt like a ghost. The game I was playing as a child, lately was tight, and I wanted to say proudly who were my parents. Even this secret would have had an expiration. And it was January 1993.

Chapter 8: Arrivederci Palermo
Goodbye Palermo

Unlike my peers, my mornings were mostly free from commitments so that I could go around Palermo or in the countryside without having to return. I account to no one.

January 15, 1993 was also a day of those, and I had arranged to go find at school a girl with whom I was dating in that period. We had an appointment at ten o'clock, in recreation time, and immediately after I would have seen myself with others in the arcade.

I was fifteen years old and Giovanni was sixteen. That was the day that cut in two my life and that I will never forget. While we were busy throwing coins on coins in one of those video games, a guy from the group joined us.

   "Why so late?"
   "I wasn't able to get out early."
   "Did your mom do it for you?"
   "No, obviously," he clarified, and took his seat at the foosball.
   "I signed myself. Whose playing?"
   "I'm on the attack!", Giovanni came forward.
   "By the way, did you hear the latest?" he asked us thoughtfully.
   "What happened?"
   " They got Riina. They said it on the bus while I was coming. "

My heart stopped. The other guys commented surprised and intrigued, while I and Giovanni looked at each other immediately with frightened eyes. For them, they had taken Riina, but for us they had arrested our father. My brother's eyes suddenly became smaller but hard, a comfort which I needed at that time. He looked at me the way my father would, as if to tell me "Stay calm. Don't get shaken. Let's go." If it hadn't been for him, perhaps I would have burst into tears. We reacted as discreetly as possible, flaunting amazement mixed with cynicism. Phrases of the type "Holy shit, really?" and "I would like to know how they did it! 'With an excuse we managed to free ourselves in a few minutes. Giovanni said he had to see a girl while I had to do an errand on behalf of my mother. With the scooters we flew home, in silence like all the times there was a worry. I was already thinking about how much it would change my life. Those guys from the group I haven't seen them since that day in the games room.

Everyone was at home. My mother was on Dad's armchair, sitting at the tip, with the straight back and shiny eyes. As soon as she heard the door close, she turned around and there she found herself standing, frightened. "Gianni, Salvo!" she yelled, and ran to meet to hug us. It was rare in my family thus freely expressing one's feelings, but in that moment of pain everyone we spread our arms to feel united and share despair. Instantly she pulled in and embraced Maria and Lucia, who still had not grasped the tragedy.

   "And now? Mom what do we do?" Cried Maria.
   "How did they do it?" cried Giovanni. "How?"
   "Don't worry, don't worry." My mother cried.

In her eyes thirty-eight years of memories that flowed fast. Totò was no longer in the house and probably he would never come back.

Later the police would find out that my parents' wedding had never been registered with the municipality, and therefore it was not legally valid. The umpteenth mockery that was corrected only a few years later, on May 8, 1995, with a signature on a sheet of paper passed under the glass, in Ucciardone. My father had taken away from him every one of his personal effects, leaving him with only the faith on the finger. For him and my mother it was the proof of their true love, the consecrated one eighteen years earlier before God. Television added every detail on the arrest and throughout the night they went forward with special services, video documents, interviews and imaginative identikits about Totò Riina. Palermo had become completely hostile and soon the house would be filled with journalists and policemen. There was only one place where the Riina family could take refuge, the only one place to feel protected: Corleone.

I had heard about Corleone for about fifteen years, but we had never been there, neither I nor my brother. It was a mythical place, described as the cradle of happiness for my parents, where grandparents and uncles never seen before lived, where the Riina and Bagarella families all had their origins. My father never set foot in Corleone because the police would capture him instantly.

"And what do we do in Corleone?"
"Is there a grandmother there?"
"And where do we live?"
"I don't want to leave Palermo. Where's dad!" cried Lucia.
"How do we do it ourselves?"
"What do we bring?"
"But where is dad now?" insisted the little ones.

My mother listened patiently and with a concentration that only a mother can have. She thought of her husband, she worried of us guys and at the same time ran all over the house to fill our suitcases with clothes and memories.

Maria Concetta had come of age for less than a month and, put to the test from the difficult situation, helped mom in a move very different from those to which we had been used to. She told us what to do and, throughout the nights we walked around the house to collect photographs and books. We filled up I don't remember how many suitcases and I completely lost sleep, to watch with the certainty that sooner or later it would be the police entered to pick us all up. Not because there was reason for it, but because at this time anything could happen. With long dark circles up to the nose and a fatigue accumulated in twenty-four hours of preparations, at fourteen thirty we were all lined up on the doorstep at wait for taxis. We needed two to transport us. and so we split for the whole trip: my mother with Maria Concetta and Lucia in one, me and Giovanni in the other. All the newspapers of Italy had not only headlined in large characters of the capture of the head of the chiefs; Totò Riina had finally been taken and now, they said, the mafia would be defeated. I still wonder today what they thought the two taxi drivers who took us away from Palermo: a woman with her four children in escape from the Sicilian capital right in a such a significant day. Maybe they had understood everything, and also for this reason he did not ask us no questions. It was winter and the sun took little time to set. When it was five o'clock in the afternoon, we turned the last corner and finally we saw it in the distance; Corleone.

Chapter 9: Una Nuova Famiglia
A New Family

Corleone appeared to me as an expanse of dense and tangled houses. The roads were already illuminated, and from some apartments the windows showed the glare of the televisions that were on.
There were no noises, except for taxi tyres who slipped into the pavement that certainly had to be many years old. The car in front, which my mother was traveling in, slowed down. Slowly we approached the country. It was twenty-three years since she had come back here, and the memory had to struggle to take shape. Slowly we slipped into a street, then in another increasingly narrow, making chicanes among the few badly parked cars here and there. On the walls of the buildings, I read obituaries, one next to the other, as if they were of the posters, while in front of the doors of many houses there were empty wooden chairs, a tacit signal to indicate to foreigners not to occupy the passage. And then there was some lady still sitting outside, almost in the middle of the street, which she watched silently the passage of men and machines.

After a last junction, at the top of the climb of St. John, the taxi in front stopped. We went down all five and, with a sense of bewilderment never tried, we remained standing with suitcases still in hand.

"Come boys, there lives grandmother," she said.

My mother sure of her memories. We followed her without saying anything, but looking around at each other, while the taxis disappeared behind the last curves. The streetlights illuminated a sequence of old houses: some renovated, still others in rough stone, on which geckos as big as my hand were walking. There was no precise logic in those buildings, one-story, two-story, some even three-story, with or without balconies. My mother headed to a door like the others and began to ring the doorbell

There was no one around, and even from inside the answers did not come. She repeated the same gesture two or three times, with greater despondency at each ring "Ninetta!" she suddenly heard. Watching from upwards and from a balcony to the side appeared a woman who will have had more or less fifty years. She looked at us enthusiastically.

"I am your cousin! You know me?"

The cousin explained to us that grandma Lucia went to grandmother Concettina, from the in-law in short, to keep her company. Our arrival slowly became news for all the whole alley of Scorsone, and relatives and friends they began to look out from the houses and the balconies to greet us and watch the scene.

I had never seen all those people, mostly relatives of the Bagarella, and one after one I had to shake hands and introduce myself. I didn't feel like it, I was just tired. The anguish of that escape joined the novelty of a place I had seen until today only in photos and in my imagination. Aunt Josepha, for a change, was in church to pray, so we had to wait the return of grandmother Lucia to be able to enter indoors. She came running, warned by friends, and as soon as she saw us from afar she began to cry. She hugged us all, one by one, as if we had always known each other, and for the first time I returned to feeling a familiar warmth.

My mother was also a little more serene, because after so many years she felt at home again, somehow protected and in any case no longer alone. The affection of that evening turned into gossip within a night. The news of our return to Corleone spread quickly throughout the country and already in the morning of January 17 it was impossible to go around without anyone not staring at us. The first visit was that of the carabinieri. The captain and marshal invited us to go with them in section to take pictures and take fingerprints: we didn't have valid identity document and we had to comply if we wanted to start a new life here. My mother was listened to for hours, then she too could go home. What the carabinieri knew the journalists came to know it also and from that morning Corleone was invaded by televisions and interviewers hunting for news.

They were Italians but also foreigners and they probed in every aspect of our lives, stopping even the aunts who could no longer get out of a quiet house. Aunt Josepha also became assaulted daily and she, in response, limited herself to saying that it was useless to stay there, because there was no one in the house. In the house instead we were all right, all five shielded, with my grandmother Lucia who went out just to do the shopping and then came home running, ignoring photographers and microphones. Rai, Mediaset, gossip broadcasts, even Life live, everyone was knocking to our door and filled the horizon of Corleone with vans and parables.

My father's photo was in all the newspapers and we spent time with our grandmother. We read books, she would tell us stories fifty years old while looking at vintage photos, before the carabinieri came to put everything upside down and take us away from even those.

Piece by piece they took away people and memories from us. Grandma told me about Uncle Leoluca, the new super wanted, uncle Calogero, soties from childhood and days in the countryside to collect mulberries. We were a new family. How new was the knowledge and my room, on the second floor of alley of Scorsone 24. On the ground floor there were aunts, old maids, which always had funny gossip or an anecdote about old people of the country.

I felt so far away those months when, in hiding, I was free to do more of what I liked - enjoying motocross around the paths of Palermo, the trips out to Rocca Busambra, the dangers of being stopped by the forest, the past mornings with Giovanni to prepare the engines.

Now I was a guy with everyone's eyes on me, and at fifteen I had to start from scratch. But before that, there was a fixed thought in my mind: to see my father again soon.

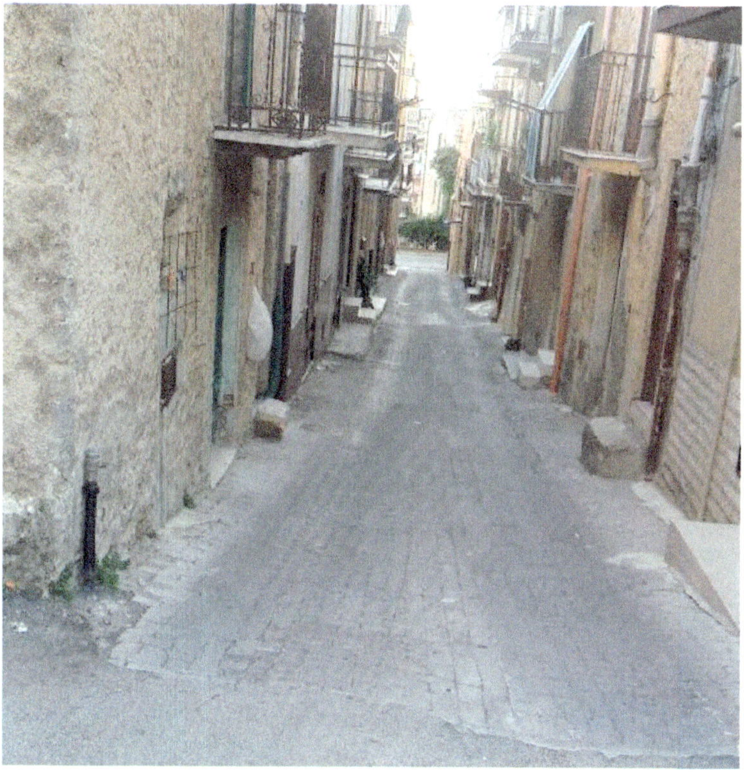

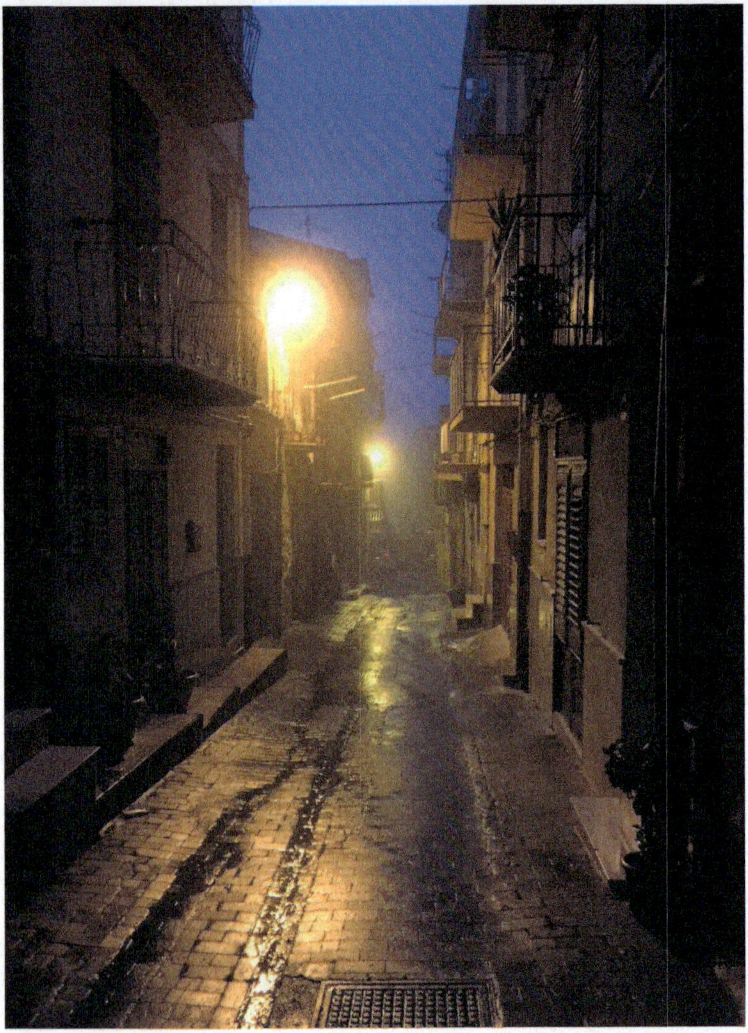

Chapter 10: Il Pianto di un Padre
The Cry of a Father

I had never taken a plane in my life. The trip I made in April 1993 became an unforgettable memory for this, too. Finally, we had permission to go to find my father and I did not know what to expect. I had never been to Rome, I had never entered a prison, I had never done a visit to a relative.

The day was hot and sunny, not like those to which we are accustomed in Sicily, however it helped to relax. We returned that same evening, and all for only one hour of visiting. The prison of Rebibbia was immense, high, severe, full of the sadness of its detainees. There were heavy red gates that closed behind us and two guards that guided us on a path always strict towards the interview room.

I saw my father every day of my life for fifteen years, from when I was born until that January 15, and I would have said I knew him well, too - I believed I knew everything about him. But that day, as soon as we found him in front of us, all my beliefs collapsed. As soon as he saw us, through the armored glass, he burst into liberating tears.

We didn't have to have beautiful faces, this one I know, but we said we would be strong and comforting. Instead, the hour passed quickly, and almost completely with tears in the eyes on both sides.

"Ninetta, how are you? Guys, what about you? And Lucia how is she?" asked Totò, seeing that the smallest was not with the group.

"She's staying at home with my mother. We are at Corleone. I didn't want to make her tired coming to Rome", replied my mother with lips that every now and then curled in, to hold back crying.

"Do I need to do something for you? Are you ok?"

"There are always journalists, always, but we're fine. In September we start school" Giovanni explained.

"Beware of people. *Quannu u diavulu t`alliscia voli l`arma*" "When the devil flatters you, he wants your soul." he specified. I looked at my father in silence. He was another man, always strong externally, but different inside. It was the first and only one time I saw him crying.

Totò Riina has never regretted his life, never needed to tell us sorry, because he always knew that we were for him and him for us. So that day, returning to the plane, I recognized that it had been a cry of love. If my father had the strength to say so, maybe that day he would have said "Excuse me". That day, looking into our eyes with a fragility hitherto unknown, he had realized that he had lost the thing forever most precious in his life.

I went back to Corleone and in September I started the surveyor's studies in Bisacquino. In Corleone there was the master's institute – where they had taught my mother – the classic one and the scientific one, but I wanted a diploma that would allow me immediately to work and not have trouble taking every day the bus.
In August my mother had gone to talk to Lino Di Vincenti, the principal of the school, attentive and helpful priest who gladly accepted my case. Neither he nor any parent had protested at my presence.

I did the exams to prove my level of education, the one matured to the sound of lessons in the kitchen, and at sixteen I was admitted to the first year of the surveyor course. I was respected by everyone, maybe for my two years older, perhaps for my personality so safe. Yet it was not easy to enter in a context such as the school one. 'Salvo, the journalists!' companions at the end of the lesson, when they rang the Bell. "They're all out here."

We Riina's lived with the presence constant of microphones and recorders, in each time of day and in every place, so my friends protected me by making me space around the crowd, up to the stop of the bus or up to the scooters. Within forty minutes I was home.

With me on the bike and Giovanni in the car, any excuse was good to be stopped from the police; we could no longer misbehave. When in the distance appeared a car stationed, we slowed down and, resigned, when side by side.
"Documents and search", the agent told us on duty, with inevitable arrogance.
"Why, what have I done?"
"Come on Riina, don't waste my time. Documents and search."

For months they checked every bolt of our cars and motorcycles, without never finding anything. There was a certain sadism in that desperate search for money, weapons and explosives. They were the "hawks" of the police, aggressive and directed in their actions, and to some they began to bother. Corleone was a country of friends and family but the situation it has become intolerable.

Chapter 11: Un Bacio e una Carezza
A Kiss and a Caress

"Salvo, isn't that Maria?" said my friend Giuseppe.
Maria? What is she doing alone?"
"It's her, look." Giovanni gave gas, starting in pursuit of that off-white "Yes" scooter.

I, sitting behind on the saddle, I was already thinking about the words to say and not to miss the occasion. She was named after my sister, Maria Concetta, and she was a beautiful and shy girl who I had met already from my first months in Corleone.

She was in different company from mine, but I often saw her in the square the evening and I did not miss an opportunity to woo her with the look. Had there been a song by Claudio Villa, as in the time of my parents, maybe it would have been easier, but I was content at least to know her and to know her name. She was always with a friend, Margherita, and, pointing out, not missed an opportunity to exchange subheading a few jokes about me. Giovanni made a sharp turn to convince her to stop. Of course, none of us had a helmet, so I could stare at myself on Maria's hair, disheveled and lit by the color of the face.

"Hello," I said to her. "Where are you going alone?"
"Nowhere. You stopped me for this?"
"Yes," I explained, under the amused gaze of my friend.
"But already that you have nothing to do, let's go for a ride together."
"You and I?"
"Why? What did I say wrong?" I said

Maria thought little about it, teased by that approach so elementary.

"That's fine. And where do we go?"
"You don't worry. But I drive," I announced.

I left Giuseppe's bike to take my place on the bike of Maria, who deviated before girding me with her arms around my waist. It was a feeling of freedom I needed in those months. I could for the first time be completely myself, because my life was clean and under everyone's eyes, and I particularly liked that girl.

I took Maria to the top of Corleone, in the abandoned villa of Pappalardo. There, taking advantage of the panorama and of the silence, I could talk to her and explain my interest with the simplicity of a teenager. A saying like *quannu la lingua voli parrari, prima a lu choirs to dumannari.* " When the language wants to speak, it must first ask the heart"
"I like you, I told you. But Margherita also likes you ", she explained to me.
"I'm just interested in you. Will you give me a kiss?" Suddenly I remembered that little girl I kissed when I was nine years old.

I knew it was time to grow up now that I was the son of Totò Riina and no more the son of Giuseppe Bellomo, and that I needed simple things to be able to free myself from pain.

Maria Concetta accepted my kiss and so, in the spring of 1994, my love story. That story that would have me accompanied for ten years, until inside the prison. I wanted to tell my father about Maria Concetta, but in those months the processes were the greatest occupation of my family, and forced us to run from one part to the other.

The flight by plane to Rome had lasted less than two hours, not as lucky was the train trip we made in May 1994 in Reggio Calabria. Five hours and forty endless minutes spent with Giovanni and with my uncle Gaetano, brother of my father, to attend the trial for the murder of Judge Antonino Scopelliti. The mafia had asked the magistrate to be more "soft" in his sentences and he, for having refused the offer, he had been killed. As always in those years, when you opened a trial for mafia, my father came punctually brought up; so we arrived in Reggio in the early afternoon, to meet with my father's new lawyer, a Calabrian. A train trip, my first ever, which I will not forget never.

Certainly, it was a mistake of the carabinieri, who did not bother to vacate the corridors adjacent to the courtroom of the trial, but it was while we were talking to the lawyer who, behind the corner, I saw a large group appear of men in uniform armed with machine guns. They walked narrow, hiding from view and surrounding, a man lower than them; that man was my father.

I Interrupted the conversation, with Giovanni and my uncle Gaetano. We flattened against the wall to allow the handpiece of soldiers to pass in front of us comfortably. Right at our height the carabinieri they slowed down and, opening slightly, discovered to my view dad. It was a surprise for both, perhaps more for him, which was dragged like a package from a part to the other without being able to expect anything again. From the day of his arrest, that was the first and only time I could see my father without the glass in the middle. That glass imposed by the isolation that transforms men into animals inside a cage. I could have reach out and touched him, if I wanted to, give him a hug. My father saw us, widened his eyes and filled with vigour. We just exchanged a greeting, and that way of looking at us comforted both. In the courtroom we were not admitted, but our prize we had already had in that way, unexpected albeit sad. My father, at the end of the Scopelliti trial, he would have been acquitted.

Chapter 12: I fratelli Riina
The Riina brothers

The bell of Santa Rosalia rang out while everyone, in an orderly line, went out from the church. The identical and monotonous chimes rumbled throughout Corleone and the inhabitants, in our passage, they discovered themselves the head and lowered the shutters of the shops. Some children ran down the street in company, but we, with a low gaze and contrite, we followed our march behind the coffin.

"They have no dignity even today," whispered Giovanni without getting distracted.

"Don't get angry, they don't understand it. These people are here to make the news," I replied.

Next to our procession was joined by a second group of journalists and cameramen that, without proving the slightest bit respectful, described the hands and faces of a normal moment of pain. Grandma Lucia who I had just met a year before and had quickly become a new point of reference for all of us. For my mother first of all, and then for us children. She could tell us everything about everyone, she was an encyclopedia living in Corleone and everyone knew her.

The whole Bagarella family was there at the funeral, on October 9, 1994, inundated with condolences and hugs of old friends. There were all but one: Uncle Leoluca. The police were looking for him everywhere and they were certain that he would also appear that day, not to give up the last farewell to his mother. The surveillance had intensified for about a month, when the rumor spread that my grandmother was seriously ill.

Aunt Angela (sister of my mother) had recently come to visit from Venezuela and, immediately after her return to America, Lucia became sick. Our phones were constantly under surveillance, and to the police it seemed providential the occasion of our pain to finally intercept Uncle Leoluca.

He had not come during the sick days, and so everyone was waiting for him at the time of the funeral. Outside and inside the church of Santa Rosalia the policemen, in plainclothes, observed faces that they had studied for weeks, and they remained silent. But a plainclothes policeman is easy to recognize: the face of a foreigner, his hands in his pockets, no one goes to greet him, often even the gun that can be glimpsed from the Pockets.

With Maria Concetta we played to recognize them and to count them. And then in Corleone every new face is immediately identified, and it is not possible to pretend to be what one is not. As per tradition, barely known of the disappearance of my grandmother, in the alley of Scorsone, became the subject of a curious procession of friends and relatives with trays and trays of food of different forms.

There were those who they brought the brioches, who the arancini, who biscotti and who breaded slices, of the good ones scented with garlic and parsley. It's a way to feel less alone, comforted by the people who care about loving you. Even on the day of the funeral we received at least ten invitations to lunch, and for a week it almost seemed like an early Christmas.

The journalists of course did not understand, they who followed us in the twentieth century procession, from a few meters away, to the municipal cemetery, where would be buried my grandmother Lucia together with other illustrious relatives.

Someone remembered to make a sign of the cross, others made close-ups of the coffin to be broadcast on all newscasts: "Dead Lucia Mondello, mother of the Corleonese boss Leoluca Bagarella and mother-in-law by Totò Riina. She was eighty-seven years old. The investigators oversee family funerals." With the disappearance of my grandmother, I had the impression that the curtain of smoke that still hid us from a part of public opinion had suddenly fell away, especially in Corleone. As if, now that she was not here, you could look at the Riina family as a separate thing. And the episodes of fury towards us grandchildren, they became more frequent. Giovanni and I knew we had to be on our guard in our words and deeds, and we tried keep as far away as possible from troubles and wrong companies, such as our father asked us.

It had already happened a few months earlier. A beautiful March morning, on the door of house of the girlfriend of the mayor of Corleone, they found a trail of blood leading on the ground: a calf's head had been thrown in the night and left there, severed, as a clear intimidating sign.

The Riinas, it was the two brothers," said the journalists to the carabinieri.

"It was to hit the mayor, it's a clear mafia signal."

"We will send the news tonight to the tg", added the representatives of the local broadcasters.

"They also did it in St. Joseph's Jato and Terrasini. All in a few weeks from the vote. To all mayors."

Giuseppe Cipriani, for all "Pippo" Cipriani, was a progressive mayor, a man put sideways with respect to the previous ones administrations and that several times had fought to build an image of the Corleonesi new and clean, far from mafia events.

It was for this reason, perhaps, that the journalists immediately said our name, starting an echo of slander that spread from mouth to mouth across the whole city.

Intimidation of this kind was unfortunately very frequent here in Sicily. Often lamb heads were used, easier to find, when you wanted to leave a last message to an enemy to convince him to the silence. Yet this time our impression was it was another: perhaps whoever had done this gesture wanted to put the population of Corleone against us, he wanted to test our reactions.

Giovanni and I were in fact kept under control not only by the police, but also by many enemies. And someone, evidently, he wanted to get a precise idea about of us. It doesn't matter if it was proven that we were strangers to this fact: for the press it was much more profitable to say otherwise.

The same happened a few months later. The morning of November 4, in the main square of Corleone, just that square that Cipriani had dedicated to Falcone and Borsellino, the marble plaque entitled to the two magistrates had been stolen.

Once again, the scandal hit Giovanni, just eighteen years old, and me. The two Riina brothers had damaged and made havoc of a symbol of the fight against the Mafia. The carabinieri intervened immediately. On November 22, the case was already resolved: it was four drunken boys who had done the damage. For fun they had pulled down the pole, breaking the plate, all without arousing the suspicions in the carabinieri, with the station at twenty-five meters from the place of the incident.

When the slab was found in the garden of the elementary school, the Finocchiaro Aprile, the names of the real guilty ones also came out. No one said, "We have wrongly accused the Riina brothers", or "Giovanni and Salvo are innocent, we should say it publicly'. Journalists were not interested in the truth and even today, when you list the faults alleged of the young Riina, the history of the plaque to Falcone and Borsellino always collects undeserved success.

Chapter 13: Una Visita Indiscreta
An indiscreet visit

"Riina, they must speak to you."
"Who is it?"
"Enter," said the guard without worrying to respond.

He turned the six locks of the isolation cell in which Totò was forced to stay in for two years, and deviated. The cell door opened, letting in more light than usual, so that my father had to cover his eyes for a few seconds, failing to glimpse the two figures who, in the meanwhile, they had brought themselves in front of him.

"Riina, how are you going?" asked the taller man.
"Nothing. I do nothing... from the morning, to the evening."
"We have come here to speak to you."
"You can ask everything. I have time."

Totò sat in the only chair of the cell, with his arm resting on the table, listening. He knew them, and he already knew the answer that he would give them.

"You know you have to cooperate. Your family needs to be protected."
"In Corleone." The other man added. "Your children."

Those words were already enough. My father, still a force in those years, stood up snapping from the chair and with his hand grabbed the metal ashtray that was on the table.

"Go away," he yelled, brandishing the object with a threatening air.

"What is this?, The market? *Accatta di quattru e vinni di ottu*?? Buy for four, sell for eight?! Go away!"

Upon hearing those cries the guard, watching at the door, opened the cell. Right away the two men came out, not at all frightened but indeed satisfied with their attempt. My father, on the other hand, had a breath.

"Goodbye, Riina", said the tallest, before returning the darkness to the high security cell.

The signals in the air said that my family still hadn't finished paying his account to justice, but my brother and I, we were trying to make our way in life as discreet as possible, as we were taught as children.

Of course, our character had changed and we conformed less than of the past. We were now real Corleonesi, all in one piece, stubborn and with that pinch of unconsciousness typical of young people. The summer of 1995 was my first as an adult.

Like every year when it arrived August the country was filled with foreigners and emigrant relatives who returned for the holidays. There were those who arrived by plane and those who arrived in car, each trying to flaunt the well-being achieved far from Sicily: the streets filled with Mercedes, BMW, girls in fashionable northern dresses and boys who felt better just because they lived in the city.

There were always many Germans, and one in particular I remember because they cost us yet another headline in the newspaper. He and a friend of mine had a soft spot for the same girl, and several times he had threatened with beatings - even in public. Things were said of all colors and I, who was happily engaged to Maria Concetta, I had of course taken the side of the Corleonesi, against the German "foreigner". '

"I picciriddi devono parrare sulu quannu piscia a jaddina" Kids should only talk when the hen is pissing," we laughed in his face, and one day, meeting him at the bar, I turned to him the eloquent gesture of the horns.
"*Prima 'i parari mastica i paroli*" Before talking, chew the words.", I added.

A few days later, the night of August, we were all dancing in a nightclub of Corleone, 'in Giarra, and I found him behind me. I was wrong, I understood it only later, but his expression and the presumptuousness of his presence... it tasted defiant, that triggered a reaction of annoyance from me.

I first hit him in the face with a fist, then with a precise kick between the legs, in the general curiosity of the people, partly scared and partly amused. The deejay rose the music to cover the consequent shouting, while the German ran away fast.

"Run as long as you want, I'll always wait for you here." I yelled at him.

It was the police who returned, and in short time. They were always in plainclothes, in half the crowd, and they were waiting for nothing else.

"Where is Giovanni Riina?"
"What does my brother have to do with it. I stand on my own.'
"Bring him here." they decided anyway.

In the meantime, the German had returned, was put in front of me, and the policeman tried to convince him on what to do.

"This guy who beat you up," he said, knowing well who I was
"He is of legal age. If you want, you can report it and we bring him right in. Think about it."

The German looked at me carefully. I think they had told him my name, and basically he didn't want any more trouble. It had been a quarrel between boys, no need to raise dust, and he said he didn't want to stick out a complaint. The policeman was visibly disappointed by this outcome.

"Shake hands," he ordered. Then, lowering the voice and approaching my ear, he added
"Be certain Riina, this does not end here."

I don't remember the name of that agent, but I remember that he was one who was looking for his photo in the newspaper at all costs. When I recognized him in the distance, at checkpoints, I knew that it would be more tiring than expected to get out of it.

"You were flying with the bike" he said one day, after surprising us two-up on the scooter.
"It was nothing. We'll be careful, don't worry." I replied.
"I decide whether to feel comfortable. License and booklet, come on."
"I don't have a booklet."
"And whose scooter is it? Is it yours, Riina?
"It's not mine, a friend lent it to me" I admitted.

I would never give the name as a matter of principle.

"And that friends name who lends for starters? Come on, to whom does it belong?"
"I don't remember."
"Okay, then it will mean that we will have to make a nice

complaint for theft. Let's go in the police station", he announced, with his eyes that shone with satisfaction.

In the police station I had to name the owner, a certain Mario, who, unfortunately for the cop, it was also one of the best friends of his daughter. He confirmed everything on the phone and I was free to go.

"We told you well this time, too, but I will accompany you home. I really want to see you take two slaps from your mother!" She obviously did not respond to the invitation, but she thanked the man and closed the door in his face.

In these months the expressions of my mother were worth a thousand words. She tried to preserve Giovanni and me from all kinds of trouble in which we could get ourselves. She loved us and, if necessary, also tried to scold us. But her voice was not that of my father, and maybe I would have needed him to make better choices.

Every meeting with the police in Corleone tasted like intimidation, and the streets had a thousand eyes, including balconies. Fortunately, the school was fine and the study helped me; of course, not as much as Maria Concetta and Lucia, who grew and studied with concentration and seriousness, but still distracted me and helped keep me out of trouble. John, on the other hand, just did not like the books. He gave a hand in the fields, but without a work permit, because no one was willing to put it in order. This is how it was, to escape among the rows of the vineyard when there was some surveillance in sight. He was twenty years old and what my mother feared, in the end it happened.

Chapter 14: Senza Giovanni
Without Giovanni

Sicily has its own times and rhythms, above all in the country. There are rites to be respected, breaks of the day that have their own sacredness and that should be enjoyed without thoughts. One of these rites was that of coffee after lunch. We all ate together: my mother, Maria Concetta, Lucia, Giovanni and I, to never lose the good habit of to feel still a united family.

After lunch it was customary, for the men of the house, to go out to the bar to have a coffee. Not because were not able to at home, but because it was a way to have a chat and joke on the latest news. The bartender was a friend, still accustomed to serving drinks only in a glass, with those teaspoons all unpaired, and discolored red chairs, lined up in front of the door, with the inscription Algida on it.

It was June 11, 1996, at about fourteen o'clock. when Giovanni and I got up from the table. Someone knocked violently on the door. Three, four bangs.

"Police. Open up." said a voice in a peremptory tone.

My mother, counting with pain the steps that separated her from that moment, she opened the door and immediately they threw themselves inside, Eight DIA policemen armed with everything. While shouting at the door he held in his hand a rigid folder on which was written the name of my brother. The road was blocked off by cars and other policemen, while the first journalists already they were beginning to arrive.

"Rest assured," Giovanni said before leaving the house. "Everything will be fine."

The accusations levelled at my brother had changed and they had grown over the years. To condemn him there were only the words of the repentants, Monticciolo and Brusca above all, and not the evidence of Italian justice.

It was said that Giovanni and I, one evening in January 1995, we felt watched and followed, and we had recognized a young, well-known owner of a clothing store on the course. The story came up to our uncle Leoluca who, to defend the grandchildren, would then execute the boy, some weeks after, on Saturday evening in the center, blatantly. It was supposed to be a clear demonstration of strength in front of everyone, the young man's sister was also killed, as well as his brother-in-law, just for being worried and have asked a few questions.

These are stories that come out of the accounts of the repentant. The repentant ones who, before becoming such, were themselves in turn murderers. So, at what time does a detestable man suddenly become the person most respectable and sincere in the world?
Giovanni was charged with these three murders, and additionally for a fourth murder he was also declared to be the perpetrator. His "baptism of fire," the journalists wrote, who could invent a reconstruction imaginative of my family, putting into it all those little slanders that we had carried with us until then: calf heads, brawls on the premises, commemorative plaques stolen and so on.

Giovanni was brought immediately in Palermo and I, suddenly, I found myself at be the only man of the house. I had understood immediately the situation, even when my mother called our lawyer to ask his advice.

He told her something bad on the phone, it was clear from the expression she gave.

"Rest assured, you wait here while I'm going up to the courtroom", he explained once they arrived in the city.

We were in Via del Fante, where notification of arrests were usually announced. We sat down for almost two hours in that corridor, with Lucia asleep on my shoulder and Maria Concetta who held our mother's hand. We looked like family members in a hospital waiting for the response of a serious operation. The lawyer went down the stairs and appeared in front of us. "Gianni was arrested. They are carrying him to the Ucciardone", he admitted.

Every day we spent in Corleone, my brother Giovanni always reminded me of my dad, with that sturdy build not exaggerated in stature, and like him he had ended up in Palermo. In 2001 he would receive the sentence to life imprisonment, confirmed in second instance in 2003 and made final by the Supreme Court in January 2005.

Since that day in June, Giovanni has never been a free man, and never again will be. That last coffee together that we never had. My mother in tears begged me not to leave her alone, who would not have made it if she had to bear another loss.

Since I was a child, my father Totò left me few, but good rules of life that are the basis of the man who I am today. Those words are what defend me especially from the stories that the so-called repentants, the "collaborators of justice" build daily on the Riina family.

"In life there is always time to repent of his own choices," he explained.

"But you are solely responsible for your conscience, so if there is a price to pay for that you have chosen, you just have to pay for it."

To repent of who we are, just to save us from jail, it is not a sign of honor, but of cowardice, especially if you have to do it by accusing other people. It's more honest a person who has consciously chosen and pays only with one's own conscience, or one who repents out of fear?

"I knew the pain very early, and I had to choose what to do to save the people I loved", he often told me my father, with a distant gaze.

"Therefore, always remembers one thing, Salvo. We do not repent in front of men, but only in front of God."

Chapter 15: Un Ricordo di Sangue
A memory of blood

My dad had stopped going to school in 1940, after obtaining the third grade, at the age of ten. As for most of the Corleonesi children, the economic hardships were little reconciled with a life of study, and he had to settle for to learn to read and write.

Corleone in those years was a real, and small town of almost fifteen thousand inhabitants, separated from Palermo through fifty endless kilometers of curves – tortuous and mostly unpaved. Troubled on a hill, there we lived on pastoralism and agriculture, and basically the work was there for everyone, but you had to roll up your sleeves.

The Riina family lived in via Rua del Piano, a very narrow downhill road in which, many years later, would become difficult to pass even a car one at the time. Every morning the baker's cart went down and, stopping at every door, distributed loaves of different sizes, while for everything else there were the shops that met going towards Santa Rosalia.

It was a tangle of narrow streets where a foreigner would be easily lost, but not he who was born and lived there. Many had been forced to emigrate, following the sad example of many municipalities of Palermo. Every afternoon my father Salvatore, for all Totò, ran up and down the street, chasing balls that rolled away too fast and marbles disputed with other children of his age.

He was the second of five children: there was Caterina, Totò, Gaetano, Francesco and Archangel. In the summer of 1943 arrived the fifth pregnancy, that of Giovanna Francesca, who would be born in winter. Totò's mornings were dedicated to fields, to help father Giovanni in sowing and in the collection, following the rhythms that the Sicilian land imposed.

In September the harvest was already over, because of the scorching sun. He soon did his job and, so that did not turn into "pàssoli", the grapes were harvesting quickly. That Day Salvatore he had gone to the country alone, because his father had reserved himself a task much more delicate. Not even a month after Operation Husky, the landing of the Americans in Sicily, the island showed clear signs of destruction. Of all the bombs fired inland, precisely on those most difficult mountain villages to be identified, many had remained unexploded. My grandfather Giovanni had found one and, victorious, he had brought it home, intending to take advantage of it: from the iron would have made a new plowshare, because the one they had was bent and rusty and there was no money to buy another. He was an extremely good man. maybe just too naïve and light with life. Unlike my grandmother Concetta, who instead often knew how to make decisions for both.

Toto was on his way home when a serious and powerful roar came to his ear, right in his direction, a roar of those he felt during the American raids. You couldn't see smoke in the distance. but the noise clearly came from the southern slope of Corleone.

He began to run madly; he was only thirteen years old and not out of breath, but his breath broke when he arrived on the spot. Via Rua del Piano was unrecognizable, full of stones and bricks scattered everywhere. The courtyard was gone, replaced by a chasm half a meter deep beyond which the screams of the neighbors came.

There were no ambulances to call in those days, and they all began to dig, to pile up debris, to avoid the beams of the ceilings that had been lay to the right and left.

"Mom! Mom where are you?" he screamed in despair did Toto.
"Toto! Totò!" cried Concetta, with a shrill voice and throat eaten by dust.
"Toto! The bomb!" she shouted.
"The bomb!"
"And dad? Where's dad?" he began to despair too.

Giovanni had been thrown some distance away on detonation. He wanted to open the bomb with the recklessness of a poor farmer who he does not think of danger but only of utility; it looked empty, no gunpowder, he had tried to break it with a stone and that had exploded before his eyes. You are never prepared for the sight of the blood, and now my grandfather looked mangled and ragged in every limb.

"And the others? Mom? Where are the others?". Totò shouted.
"I don't know! I don't know!" she screamed, bursting in an infinite cry while with her hands tightened around her belly, now at the sixth month stage of pregnancy. In tears she slumps on what was left of the small bench stone of the courtyard.

Another five meters further, Totò saw the sheets of metal lying on the ground, and under the flap of a T-shirt. "I beg you!" he asked a boy older than him, who was re-governing his animals who were naturally agitated. The show was even more gruesome. Under the panel was a motionless little body, with the belly open by a splinter. The torn shirt and shorts, shorts of those who at that time were probably playing and running in front of the house. It was Francesco, the youngest brother, of seven years, lifeless and without the possibility of help. My father walked away horrified, then he ran to look for the other brothers. Catherine and Archangel were inside the house at the time of the explosion, safe, immediately overlooked on what was left of the entrance and now embraced their mother. They all three sobbed, but at least they were safe. Gaetano, on the other hand, was not crying. When Totò he reached his little brother and saw that he was silent, with his gaze fixed forward, in shock.

"What are you doing? Tano? What's wrong with you?", as he shook him. He didn't speak, but he held his hands tight on his foot, to hold back the pain, dirty with blood and topsoil.

"Let me see, Tano. Don't be scared." The fall of one of the fixtures of the façade of the house he had cut his big toe, and now bled conspicuously through the leather of sandalwood. It took a lot of bandages and many stitches in the hospital to stop the bleeding. Sometimes we think that a certain age is enough or a diploma to understand when we are mature, but this is not the case. You grow when fate decides it.

We had not made war, the American bomb that remained unexploded, and the Riina family found itself in front of a radical change. Now it was Totò who was the man of the house, only thirteen years old, and his was the task of keeping the family going. My aunt Caterina, the eldest, had fifteen years, up to the newborn Giovanna Francesca, who never knew my grandfather. "Praying to God and working" were the rules that my father gave himself, while grandmother

Concetta, from that day dressed in mourning, she dedicated herself to small housework jobs to earn some extra money.

Totò was the soul of the Riina family for six full years, until 1949, the year of the first arrest. They played with other friends at the club of bowls when, out of the blue, burst a violent firefight. He didn't back down from defending his friend, and there was an exchange of shots with another guy. Both were injured by the shooting, my father he managed to find assistance in a nearby house. From there it all began, at just eighteen years.

"Always choose your friends well", he told me, a lesson taught by my father.
"As I did."
"Why, Dad, how did you choose them?"
"You have to choose only the best people, the ones you can learn from. Walk with those."

It was his motto. Even today, often, I wonder if I have kept to his advice.

Chapter 16: Tentativi di Futuro
Attempts at the Future

Exactly two years had already passed since the arrest of my brother Giovanni, and I in June 1998, I finally graduated as a surveyor. Now that the school had finished being my alibi, I had to start worrying about what I would do with my life.

The university it was not at the top of my desires, I wanted to be active right from the start. I wanted to test myself in the world of work. I took a Sabbatical year to understand what the right choice was.

The wait bore fruit and I was convinced I wanted to open my own business of a commercial type together with a dear friend. If I was going to be a member of the world, it was necessary to have a piece of paper, so we attended a course of three months in Palermo. When I obtained the regional certificate of commercial agent, I returned immediately to Corleone. It was 2000 and finally I could start working.

We started as representatives at some local businesses. Our task it was to place the grain of the small companies with large companies that had need to "cut" their own production. In Sicily we were used to this phenomenon, and always our land has been subsistence to industries, often north, which strengthened their poor products with our extraordinary materials first. Wine is one of the greatest examples of this.

"Have you finished commuting?" asked Roberto Consiglio, owner of a machine dealership agricultural in Agrigento.

"I like to travel."

"Do you like to be a door-to-door salesman? Instead, I'll make you a proposal."

"All right. I'll listen to you."

"You're from Corleone, right? And in Corleone who is there who deals with agricultural machinery? Nobody. I need to enlarge my business also in other areas of Sicily. If you start to be a representative just for me, you can do great business."

Corleone had a great vocation and I wanted to reduce my travels and learn new things. I accepted the proposal, and with my partner, I took a large shed right at the entrance to the village. I supplied the machine showroom of the company Agrimar and I convinced myself that I knew how to do it.

Soon we had to overcome even the anti-mafia certificate problem. The documents to be produced were extensive and the harassment towards me was as well. The certificate was a dream, even if my criminal record it was clean. I had to resort to lawyers to get satisfaction and win the hearing. For every step forward I took in my life there was someone trying to limit me. I have always preferred that they should be the lawyers to speak but, in those years, also they seemed uncertain.

I had the impression that they made little effort, as if on Palermo had suddenly fallen a strange halo of perennial suspicion for anything I did. I, who coincidentally was the only one man of the Riina family still free. In truth, there was also uncle Gaetano, brother of my father, the miracle from the explosion of 1943.

He was a very practical man, white hair and hollowed cheeks, with intelligent advice and available to listen to us grandchildren. He lived in Mazara del Vallo, but came often to Corleone to visit us. One of the last times I saw him, before my arrest, was September 7, 2001, at the wedding of my sister Maria Concetta.

It was important to have also my uncle close, on that feast day, to endure the emotion of the moment. The night before the wedding came my cousins, and according to a happy habit, we washed the whole street with water. Went early to dinner, to prepare for the great day, and I remember like that night, between a chat and a laugh, the house was filled with good mood as there had been none for a long time. Journalists did not stop accompanying us even that day, trying to browse everywhere. I took my sister under her arm and then I accompanied her in front of the altar, where Tonino was waiting for her.

When I tell the difficulties and constraints of what my life as a son was subjected to, I never forget the sacrifices that the women of the Riina house have also made.

Maria she met her future husband in 1995 and also he, because of his acquaintances with my brother Giovanni, was subjected for three years under special surveillance, from 1997 to 2000.

Lucia, who would have married in 2008. She was still the little girl at home, and the most defenseless. She had to give up studying art in Palermo because her last name did not allow her to move on her own in freedom, and so she continued to cultivate her dreams as a painter in Corleone.

For the wedding lunch we moved to a villa and there we finally managed to unmark ourselves of journalists, kept at a distance from the owner of the room. We ate, we laughed and we danced until the speaker, who was mixing a record while the tambourine was played, did not take the floor.

"Please gentlemen, a minute of your attention. The Riina family asked me to read you something that arrived last night from Ascoli. Yup, it is a telegram from Salvatore Riina addressed to these newlyweds. "

Even the last guests who were still talking stopped to listen.

Dear Mari, my adored daughter, and dear Tonino, unfortunately I'm not there today to celebrate the day that any father dreams of seeing. I wish you all the good possible for a serene and full life of blessings. I'm far away but I'm close to you with the heart. Congratulations. Salvatore Riina

Everyone burst into spontaneous applause. I saw Lucia squeezed mom harder, who was clearly upset. My father always had the right words for us children. Those who do not know it would say that he is a silent man, but not to us.

If he had spoken more, even as a recluse, perhaps it would not have been the lightning rod on which so many repentants were able to slam freely their own accusations. Cangemi, for example, had recounted that in 1989 Brusca and Salvo Madonia had started a drug trade without permission of my father, and for this they had been initially sentenced to death, but then a subsequent rethink.

Maybe it's from that moment that was born hatred and desire to Brusca's revenge against my family. Not content to hit my dad, it also involved Giovanni, some years later. Among the accusations was one that of having seen my brother wielding weapons at the age of five years old, during a meeting between bosses. Never did our father carry a weapon inside the home, let alone put it in the hands of one of us children!

The day of celebration for Maria Concetta ended with a last toast at midnight. Then we all went back to our houses, while the newlyweds would leave quickly for their honeymoon in Morocco.

I couldn't get to sleep that night. I was happy but contemplative while I turned on the mattress, looking around in the dim light, I lingered my eyes on the Giovanni's empty bed. I missed him terribly. I thought back to that episode that I had told my father, of that visit received in the cell, and I understood that soon things would get even worse. The Riina brothers were perfect prey for family enemies. Hit us to hit Toto, hoping to make it soften and to make him speak – or not to speak, depending on of the necessities. They did not succeed, and for this we were not spared.

Chapter 17: Gli occhi della polizia
The eyes of the police

I remember well the last visits made to Giovanni and to my father, because jail has given me so much time to think and to rebuild situations and words. When the whole day passes without doing anything you can get out of it in only two ways: going crazy or learning to remember. Thus, on the threshold of my last days as a free citizen, I continued to lead a quiet life, at home with my mother and with Lucia.

The first months of 2002 had begun with strange sensations, the same ones that had last preceded with the arrest of my brother. Everywhere I went I felt observed. At the bar, on the street, in church or at the barbershop. I had eyes on me, more than just the usual ones, like some of the journalist who occasionally popped up for an exclusive interview. I was leaving the car parked and on my return, there were plainclothes policemen staring at me, I accompanied the aunts to the market, and another couple of men followed me.

The confirmation came to me in March, during one of my usual visits to Giovanni. At that time my brother was detained in Calabria, in the prison of Palmi. Every round trip of course was to the burden of the family, so that morning, as always, I started driving early to make the four hour drive it took to arrive.

When we were not yet in Messina, I had to stop to get gasoline. I made the usual walk to the motorway restaurant, right for a coffee, but, as soon as we got to the checkout, I stopped horrified.

"Just a coffee?" asked the cashier.
"No. Excuse me," I replied leaving the queue.

I headed in front of the mobile newsstand on the which were hung numerous newspapers. Immediately above the sports ones there was a newspaper (a very famous national), and on the front page there was my picture. They had to have it taken shortly after my arrival in Corleone, because I still had my face as a kid. But the most worrying thing was the writing which dominated the side: "Secret inquiry on the young Riina". "Giuseppe Salvatore Riina", said the article, "is the subject of investigations on money laundering and collusion with the mafia. The scion of the Riina family lives in Corleone since January 1993..." and continued with the usual biography.

I bought the newspaper, doing the unusual gesture to fold it in two to hide my photo from the eyes of the cashier. Then I went out. The walk from the auto-grill to the car was one of the most desperate moments of my life.

I had been slammed on the front page, without knowing anything beforehand, without a word from the police, except for suspicions that I had in those months. That would have really been the beginning of the end. If they had also involved me, if I had been swallowed up by inquiries and processes like my father and my brother, the family would have crumbled altogether.

My thoughts moved to Maria Concetta, my girlfriend, who knows how she would react. I couldn't keep it a secret, even for I would have immediately spoken to Giovanni about it, And, as soon as I got in the car I showed the newspaper to my mother.

"Look what it says," I said, and I passed it to her. She read it in silence.

"Okay," she concluded.

"But where do these come from here, but what news is it?"

"Rest assured now. It's gossip." She added. She didn't want to see, but read on my face all the pain compressed in a grimace of rejection. "Now let's go, otherwise it will be late."

I called the lawyer from the ferry itself, while we waited to go down to Calabria. He didn't know anything either, it had to be news that has escaped from someone's hands. Probably this investigation was still in progress, and a journalist too bold had it published. If that is the case, then it was even more disturbing.

Meanwhile, behind us, the police had boarded the ferry. They did not stop following me step by step. Palmi prison is a bit like all Italian prisons: cold, dilapidated, steeped in sadness and, in the case of Giovanni's section, also of resignation.

In 2001, in fact, he had been sentenced to life imprisonment, and this cut the legs from underneath us. Life imprisonment is of no use to anyone: it doesn't "cure" you, it doesn't offer a ransom, it doesn't help you in anyway, not even to die. You watch yourself turn off a little at a time. You consume yourself without being able to be useful in anything, neither to you nor to society.

"It's not better the death penalty at this point?". an inmate once told me during the hour of freedom. It was a final sentence of life imprisonment, that of Giovanni, but the lawyer had tried to have him commuted to thirty years of imprisonment, thanks to the applicable shortened rite according to the Carotti law. Unfortunately, the story showed us that this, in the case of my brother, it was not possible. In 2014 he was refused the appeal. Giovanni is still there.

They finally admitted us to the visiting room, from one side my brother on a chair, on the other the three of us on the bench. Next to us, to right and left, other families who have come here to greet their loved ones; between us and them a little transparent plastic screen. The things to eat that my mother gave him that she had prepared, we had left them at the entrance, just before the search. Stuffed in a large mailbox, these packets are analyzed with care and then get to the detainee at the end of the interview. Giovanni was excited to see us, and his voice was particularly energetic.

"Salvo, what's wrong? You have a face," he told me.

"I'm fine, Gianni. You received your pajamas that we sent you? The newest ones."

"Leave the pajamas alone, Salvo. What's going on?"

"Bad story, My Gianni", said my mother. She always vented with my brother.

"There was an article this morning in the newspaper."
"Where is it?"

"They kept it at the entrance. Anyway, says they have opened an investigation into me. One of their own."

"Fuck." It got dark.

" Whatever. You don't give a shit. You just be careful, be good. What do you do... You know they're not waiting for anything else."

"I know", I replied.

We talked about a few other things that day. We showed him all the photos of the wedding of Maria Concetta, because we hadn't looked at them with him, we could show them all, and we did. We laughed over some of the gossip and some anecdote that our uncle Gaetano had told us.

The two hours passed quickly, and it was already time to get back on track for Corleone. Visits in a prison are a moment extraordinary for those who understand psychology. I have lived them as a visitor and as the visited, and I discovered many things. For example, I have discovered that the moods are perfectly reversed between before and after. Before the interview the prisoner is always tense, nervous, has performance anxiety of who must pretend to be well so as not to afflict relatives. You need to wash your face well, not have dark circles, smile a lot.

A euphoria very similar to those who go to visit and know of having to give his all. After the visit the opposite happens. The prisoner has a free heart, he has the face of his dearly loved imprinted in mind, he took all the positivity to go on until the next visit. But at that point those who suffer it is the family, as we suffered in that moment, returning home, mentally exhausted, as well as physically.

You leave a piece of your heart in that cage and you will see it again maybe in two weeks, hoping that he will have always the strength to fight. Things don't get better with hard jail time, when even the voice that comes to you is counterfeited by the metallic sound of an intercom and contact is prohibited from a glass in the middle, often several Cm thick. We had four hours a month to use for visits: twice for two hours. It was March 2002 and that was one of the last times when I would see my brother.

Chapter 18: Totòs
Totos

To go and visit my father the trip it was longer. Totò Riina was detained in those years in the prison of Ascoli Piceno, isolated in a maximum prison. The hard jail had cut him off from the world, and not only from the outside: isolation inside a cell with an independent bathroom, a ban on eating with other detainees, deprivation of all work programs to make himself socially useful. My father could be with no others, only with himself.

Once a month, as mentioned, you are entitled to a visit of up to one hour or, alternatively, to a ten-minute phone call. The phone call must be made between the prison of the inmate and the prison closest to the family member that you intend to call. So, my mother, who in those months could not go to Marche, was forced to go up to the Ucciardone of Palermo to be able to talk with her husband.

My last visit was in May 2002. By now I was used to taking planes. Overcoming the fear of air voids of the first times, so I flew to Rome and from there I continued by car to Marino del Tronto, eight kilometers from Ascoli.

I remember the endless journey along the via Salaria. In the stops I was always terrified to find new surprises on some daily, but since that episode in March in fact, nothing more had been known about the famous "secret investigation".

I found Dad very changed. Almost ten years had passed since his arrest, and white hairs had increased. Grizzled, he wore prescription glasses now, but had kept the red cheeks that made me laugh so much as a child.

"Dad, how are you here?"
"*Mah, ci fici 'u caddu*. Ah, you get used to it. The jail is all equal.'
"Have you read the newspapers I sent you?"
"But what newspapers, Salvo. The eyes fall on me, puppets, puppets, puppets. I am old.'

It is true, in prison time passes more slowly, but age advances faster. My father's eyes had become grayer and more off. I noticed it but didn't say anything.

"And Lucia? How is she?"
"At home. Always drawing."
"Good Lucia, she keeps herself good. And you, Salvo" he looked at me carefully, slowing down the words,
"Do not take the sword more than the tip. Be careful. *A megghiu parola è chidda ca nun si dici.* " The best word, is the word you don't say."

Without me saying anything, my father had already understood everything. He repeated to me once again to be careful with certain people, to avoid certain contexts because it took little to look like I was into trouble. Everyone was now looking at me, and I didn't have to do "minchionate".

Since I started my second life in Corleone I had grown up and I became a man. I had travelled, I had had fun with friends, I had seen places, but in the end I always came back to my house. I did not feel the need to escape from my land, as perhaps instead was suggested by my father.

Outside Sicily my name has always made me followed, and I never thought of hiding it, although this would have avoided me many comments afterwards. The people who knew me and read the surname Riina always scrupulously asked who I was, and almost did not believe in hearing the kinship.

Memory of a holiday in the Balearic Islands with friends. There were some problems with the flight and we were forced to postpone the departure by a couple of days. So, I went to the agency of travel and submitted my documents for registering our ticket.

"This is your document?" asked the beautiful girl with black eyes sitting at the desk in front of me. I thought I had done it now.
"Yea, it's me. Why?"
"You're Riina Giuseppe Salvatore? Riina with..."
"Yes, Salvatore Riina. My father."
"Really? The famous Totòs Riina!" exclaimed with a certain malice.

I had never heard of my father called "Totòs", but the truth is that is the name that he is known all over the world, many who to hear it still remain today affected. I had had a singular test also a few years earlier.

It was spring of 1996 and I was nineteen years old. In that period, I often went to dance with friends and that evening we were in an open-air disco near Bisacquino. We were a very large group. While we were dancing a friend of mine came up to my ear.
"Salvo!" he yelled, trying to overpower the noise of the music.
"Davide, what is it?".
"Salvo, I met one. He says he is the son of your father."
"What?"
"Yes, he presents himself to the people."
"Take me to him." I ordered.

I had known many mythomaniacs, but this story of this half-brother was new and intrigued me. We approached a group of boys and Davide pointed the culprit out to me.

"Hello," I said. "Can I ask you who you are?"
"Why, what do you want?"
"They told me something and I wanted to know if it was true."
"I understand", he admitted with a certain arrogance.
"Yes, I am the son of Totò Riina." I looked at him annoyed, trying to hold back any rash reaction.
"Listen to me, I think you're wrong" I explained. "I am Riina's son. So, if my father went with your mother and you are a bastard son, this I would know. But I do not know of these results."

The boy, maybe a little older than me, at first he went rigid, in a sense of defiance. But then he looked around, and noticed the sarcastic expressions of my friends who they were standing by my side. He understood that you do not answer a lie with another lie, and that evidently I was telling the truth. He became flush.

"Fuck, excuse me ... But it was just a joke! It's done, it's done! Can I offer you a drink?"
"But what to drink," I replied. "forget it, it won't happen again." While he was still sweating cold, I went back and resumed my evening. I was certain that such a thing would never be repeated again.

The day in Ascoli Piceno passed quickly, but when I arrived in Corleone it was already late: twelve hours of travel for just an hour of conversation. It was in the May of 2002 and I should have waited another month before seeing my father again. In the meantime, I would have been content to look at him in photos. In the house we only had some, a couple dating back to before 1993, of those saved ourselves from police search of 17 January. The photos after 1993 are not sincere, although one always keeps one inside the wallets, near the santino of San Leoluca, patron saint of Corleone. The ones that shoot you in prison are fake photos, you force yourself to smile in order to send them to family members and prove that you are still alive, but there nobody falls. And in the end I also became like those photos: gray and with the stench of jail on me.

Chapter 19: Terremoto alle 2:37
Earthquake at 2:37

On the evening of June 4, 2002, I had a great time playing soccer with friends. I learned to play ball with Giovanni since we lived as fugitives and then, arrived in Corleone, the weekly game with other friends it had become a date permanent. We went to eat a pizza all together and we commented on action by action under the bored eyes of our girls who, instead, had spent the whole meeting sitting in the stands talking about their problems.

It was an evening like many others, it ended after that and I had accompanied Maria Concetta to the house. We've been together for eight years now, and the aunts asked me one day why I hadn't got married yet.

"Cu lassa a strata vecchia pà nova sapi 'nzoccu lassa and a sapi 'nzoccu attrova" *"He who leaves the old way for the new, knows what he leaves but does not know what he finds"* I replied just for the sake of annoying them. It was one o'clock at night when I turned off the light. Not even time to start dreaming when a repeated series of bangs made me open wide eyes.

They beat insistently. From below, I think. Still lost I succeeded just to sit on the bed. I turned to the alarm clock and I began to understand: the clock digital marked 2:37. Not a minute more, not one less. The violence of the blows had become such as to make the window shutters shake, so I determined to look out on the stairwell.

My mother was there, already standing and listening like me, with terrified eyes that I will never forget. I felt that even my aunts had gotten up, and I worried about the fright that Lucia would have taken. Lines on the landing going down the stairs two by two, and I opened the door wide.

"Good evening." In front of it was a policeman. And behind him many others. They were of the Captured Squad of Paermo Vicolo Scorsone was illuminated to day from the flashing lights of the cars, all parked in a row in front of the house.

Some were starting to look out from the balconies, while my mother had joined behind me. Without me being able to say or prevent anything, five agents threw themselves into the house, forcing me to back off. Seemed they knew where to go, some in the kitchen, some in the living room, some in the bedrooms. Looking for money, watches, and who knows what other treasure; but they would come back empty-handed.

While the others started the research, the man who had welcomed me with an unlikely "good evening" slipped from under the arm a briefcase of the green ones that unfortunately I had already known. "Giuseppe Salvatore Riina?" he asked, from practice. Inside the briefcase there was a huge photo at full page with my face in black and white. The same one they had used in the newspaper. "It's me," I nodded. The policeman lowered the tone, in the sense of comprehension. He had seen the anguish of my mother, her hands shaking.

"Riina, did you understand? We must arrest you. Do as I tell you," he added.
"We do without fanfare."
Unlike Giovanni, who had passed for the DIA of Palermo, I would have gone directly in the police station.

Lucia, who slept in her room that night with my mother, she finally reacted to the hustle and bustle and to the foreign presence inside the house, and she looked out from the railing of the stairs.

"Salvo, what happens? Mom, what do they want?"
"Come back to the room, Lucia", begged my mother.
"No!" yelled Lucia with all the force that she had in her body.

I had never seen her like this, agitated and desperate. I feared that for a moment she could become ill. She was twenty-two, always polite, and measured in everything, now she cried with a voice not her own.

"Him too? You're taking him away too?"
"Lucia, stay calm! I beg you!" Wept my mother.
"Not him too! Please, no!", and she ran to hug me.

She squeezed me hard, hard enough to take away my breath. I was like the keystone of my family, and now everything would come crashing down.

"Take some things to bring," suggested the policeman. I got dressed in a hurry – I was still in my pajamas – and in the first bag I found I put the bare minimum for at least a couple of nights. I signed the green card, then I was handcuffed for the first time in my life.

"Let's go Riina," he said.

I kissed my mother and Lucia, then I followed him outside. Even with the head enough, I recognized the faces of all the neighbors who witnessed the scene, how I saw the despair of my loved ones - aunts, looking out with their heads outside the door, in tears. Two agents in front, then me, and two others behind. They opened the back door for me of the car and they sat me down.

"Riina, before leaving we must pass by his car", said the policeman with the briefcase.
"In my car? And what are you doing to it?"
"Nothing. We have to take it away."
"But what are your findings? The recording system?"
"Exactly," he admitted.
"He understood."
"I understand," I thought to myself.
"I understand things which are like the top of a snare"

Yes, it was like the snare and the spinning top, when played with it's that wraps around the neck and, with a one tug, you let yourself jump away for dozens of pirouettes: I was spinning around without control, intended sooner or later, to collapse.

Chapter 20 Il Canile della Sicilia
The kennel of Sicily

I spent those other few hours of the night in the police headquarters of Palermo.

I was not alone: together with cars that escorted me there were dozens more, a procession of prejudiced arrested all in the same night, forty-four to be exact. They called that 'Operation: New Generation'. Sometimes I wonder who it is that put with so much imagination to invent these names every time there is a maxi investigation.

In Palermo they presented me with a volume of paper of a few pounds of weight. They dropped it on the desk in front of me with a great rumble. One thousand two hundred pages of arrest warrant, the entire file of the accusations drawn up by the GIP.

"Do you want coffee and croissant?" asked one of the two policemen who were accompanying me in the room. There was an impressive coming and going of soldiers passing through the corridor in front of the door.
"No, thank you," I replied. I was alienated, sleepy, let alone if I was going to eat like I were at the bar.
"What's up, do you compliment me?"
"His friends took them anyway," said the second. Who knows who "my friends" were.

They took my fingerprints, then I moved on to photos. Those photos that tomorrow would have busied the front pages of all the newspapers of Italy. Waiting to be registered and sorted in section, like the others arrested, they took me in one of the symbolic places of this hell called Ucciardone: a place that the inmates themselves renamed "the kennel". And actually, the difference between us and the beasts became very thin.

I was pushed into a square bunk, no more than one and a half meters per side, a box where you should wait a couple of hours and instead you often get trapped for five times that. The kennel is an open-air sewer where the roof is dirty plastic and the walls they are made of bars so dense that they do not pass almost no light at all. You hang on to the blind to have some air. Here you have to do everything, including needs, in a squat hidden by a high wall half a meter. From the bunks next to it you can hear people crying. I got in there at seven in the morning, I went out eight hours later.

"What should I do here?" I asked.
"You have to wait," a guard replied through the door slot.

Sleep made me close my eyes and, despite the sweltering heat, I felt the chills of fatigue. There was a bench of iron as narrow and as long as one of the sides of the kennel, and I tried to lie on it huddled, trying not to fall. Not that I had anything soft to lean on, because the floor was a simple range of cement – also rough. The only thing that I owned was my folder of one thousand two hundred pages.

I placed it at the end of the bench and I used it as a pillow. I slept, got up, then sat down again. Sometimes lying down, in a restlessness and suffering constants that no one, not even the worst of the detainees, you may deserve it. Anyway, I thought, out of the kennel the worst of it would have passed. But I was just at the beginning.

At three o'clock they came to pick me up. Walking, I curved with my back in pieces, and I was led to do the medical examination first and then in the New Joints office. I was propelling myself without understanding anything, as if I were a spinning top.

In the New Joints office, I received a sack bloated with stuff. "It's the pillowcase of the pillow," seeing my perplexity the second-in-command told me. "Inside there's everything you need."

Waiting to go to the section, I sat down on the ground against the wall and began to study the contents of my kit: sheets – stained, of course – training kit, sponge, toothbrush.

   "Riina, let's go", they ordered.

It was the seventeenth hour of 5 June 2002 when I was placed in the isolation cell. Yesterday, at this same time, I was going to play soccer with Corleone's friends. The Ucciardone is a Bourbon era prison and as such it can never, ever be suitable for modern inmates, whatever are the restoration works undergone. I finished in the famous IX section: from a kennel I was passed to a tomb. The cell was cramped, made inside of a large arch, with thick walls of at least one meter. The broken and marked floor, cleanliness was not even thought about. The steel squat smelled, it was gray and rusty, it made me sick just looking at it. The window was small and at the top, I had to put myself on the chair to look out, and you could see Palermo from its worst side: no sun, no sea, no perfumes. On the gratings was mounted a very dense net, but not enough to hold back insects. I confused day with night, because the light was very little, and to remind me of it there were only the screams of the guards and the buzz of mosquitoes. It was impossible to sleep, despite the tiredness: I had never heard mosquitoes so loud, so much so that I hid under the sheets all the way over my hair, sweating to no end.

These were the days of the World Cup in Korea and Japan. The matches, because of the time zones, they aired in the morning, but in my cell there was nothing, let alone television. I sensed something when I heard the lucky cell neighbors, who could follow the National team at least by radio. I remember that the first thing I asked my lawyer when I saw him a few days after on June 13 were the details of the Mexico-Italy match. I wanted to know how Inzaghi had played, back from his first year with the shirt of my Milan. One to one: we had moved on to the eighth round. And while Byron Moreno cheated all of Italy in the famous football match with South Korea on 18 June, I was made aware of the charges along with who had been arrested. They pitted them one by one, and they would ask fourteen years and six months imprisonment.

I was accused of being the leader of a group of persons interested in public contracts, in particular to some business related to the port of Palermo. Then there was an attempt to extortion, damage to public property, illegal carrying of weapons and two further accounts of attempted extortion. They had put everything in and, since there was talk of association and use of weapons, my charges fell under the article 416-bis: I was accused, ultimately, of association mafia-like. Contrary to what many wrote in newspapers, in the charges, not even once, did the name of my family members appear. Giovanni Riina was not cited, let alone the "head of the chiefs" Totò Riina. In 2004, the Court of First Instance of the minors of Palermo entered me in the register of suspects for the trial on the murders for which my brother was convicted. You've never seen a court of law of this type ask for twenty-seven years of imprisonment, however I have been fully absolved.

While waiting for the first appeal I was trying to find my way at the Ucciardone, and I wondered how well my family members had done to have passed through those same places. How did Giovanni smile when we went to see him? How did my father manage to smile even if just in photography? The first visit was traumatic.

> "You came," I said, staring at my mother and Lucia.
> "Of course we came. How are you, Salvo? How do they treat you?"
> "Mom, how do dad and Giovanni do it? How do you manage to stay here?"
> "Get strong. You will see that you will be out soon."
> "I still can't even use things I would normally use at home. I have to go on with the only shirt and the only pants they gave me. I consume liters of soap.'

We laughed about it, Lucia first. She was always teasing me because I was fixated with the clothes and I liked to have everything clean and accurate. That laugh lightened my heart, even the PM, at the first hearing, I was fixated on my shirt that I hadn't been able to wash.

> "And what is that, Riina? Is it blood?"
> "But what blood, your honor! It isn't!" They could see everything and the opposite of everything when it came to us. How much ink they wasted on the family Riina!

Chapter 21: Le montagne profumano
The mountains smell

The years of imprisonment decided by a court are like an auction. A downside for defenders, an upside for prosecutors. The first degree provided a fourteen year and six months sentence. At the second appeal they gave me twelve years. Finally, after the last appeal, the Supreme Court has fixed the penalty at eight years, enjoying an additional discount thanks to the fact that the accusation of association Mafia had been shot down under ten. The President, however, wanted to add his own, adding up another ten months. Total sentence: eight years and ten months. But they were not all continuous, because my trip into the prison system was just beginning. The fear of receiving a life sentence or falling into some bureaucratic trap that cannot be averted, but I believed that sooner or later I would get out of jail, and that was the only stimulus that allowed me to stand it in there. The feeling that I still was kept in the prison is that of an exclusively punitive function, and never educational. For each what was needed the "domandina": to have a phone call, have a T-shirt, be able to take a shower, receive a medical examination. "Riina Giuseppe?" called the guard from the outside and opened the armored door.

> "What's up?" "Come out, the appointee must speak to him. He is transferred" I smiled at the idea of the verb "transferred" and I stood up.
> Transferred? And where?"
> "He doesn't care. Prepare his things and get out", he ordered.

I picked up the few clothes I had with me and I slipped them into the usual red canvas bag and followed the agent. They escorted me to the exit, where two more plainclothes agents were already waiting for me. I signed the delivery sheet, just like you do with parcels, and they put it in a yellow envelope. With the corner of my eye I succeeded to read the header. It said: House of imprisonment of Sulmona. It was the morning of June 29th In Punta Raisi we took the plane to Rome, where, when we landed, an armored car awaited us with others and two escort policemen. For a moment the good mood returned to me.

The Sun invited me to a hint of a smile and, after over twenty days of Ucciardone, it didn't seem true to me to be able to look outside and breathe some good air. The armored car went on the A24 and began the two-hour journey to Abruzzo. From the roof I could see the sky, albeit veiled by the grid, and even the first mountains Apennine. That barren landscape and solitary made me hope for my future, although it was only at the beginning.

The prison of Sulmona had nothing to do with what can be seen with the Bourbon prison from which I came from, with high roofs and all gray. Here there was a green color that softened the environments and appeased the view, united to a sense of order and cleanliness it was definitely more bearable. Sight was the greatest comfort I could enjoy. The window was not at the top, but at man height, and gave a view on the Majella, in an expanse of meadows and mountains that in winter they were often tinged with white. When I didn't read or rest, I spent hours watching outside and to hear sounds other than those of Sicily but equally regenerating: crickets, swallows, some owls and, above all, a fresh and clean wind. When they opened the door to give me lunch, I was waiting for the present to pass and I was breathing deeply.

"What is wrong, are you disoriented?" asked the intrigued agent who led me the first time in my new cell. He saw my expression of happy amazement. Section V of the prison was a long corridor with just twenty-five cells in a row. And it seemed even clean!

> "I'm not used to it," I admitted. Then I tried to seize the ball.
> "You can talk with the inspector?"
> "Do you need anything, Riina?"
> "You see, I have a great favor to ask of you."
> "Tell me. If we can help we will do it."
> "Tomorrow morning there is the final of the World Cup, and I'm passionate about football. Would I be able to see the match?"
> "The use of the common room is not allowed to detainees in high security, you should know that."
> "I know, but if you wanted to ask the inspector, maybe there is a way to make a small tear to the rule. Only for Brazil-Germany, that's it."
> "I'll try, but I don't promise you anything" concluded the agent with a manner that by now I had almost forgotten. Then he pointed to the cell and closed the door...

The next morning, June 30, 2002, immediately after lunch two guards showed up in the room with a blank TV that was black with at least fifteen years old. The keys they were half broken, and they placed it on a shelf at the top, where I could not get to it easily. They turned it on at one o'clock, exactly for the start of the game, and turned it off at the stroke of the ninetieth minute. For those who are in isolation every source of information with the outside world, if unauthorized, must be prohibited, thus the agents had even bothered with turning off the TV during fifteen minutes of interval, prohibiting me from advertising and flash news.

I learned about the procedures to be able to call my father and brother, who in the meantime, in July, had been finally transferred to the prison of Spoleto with the 41- encore. Marche, Umbria and Abruzzo: the three men of the Riina family had never been so close after ten years, yet to none of which we were given to see each other. There was a special consideration for those who, like me, were in this particular section of the prison of Sulmona. There were no common criminals and both with the guards and among the detainees we were treated with due respect. Once a month I received the visit of my mother and my sisters who, had been forced to add a stage in addition to the visit to my father and Giovanni. They brought me news from Corleone, of my friends, aunts. Maria Concetta told me she was waiting for the birth of her child, making me for the first time an uncle. She would have had three in all: Marialucia, Gabriele and Giansalvo – names that already to pronounce them said everything about us. She told me about how the wedding was going, where she had put the carpet that I had given for the wedding, of her attempts to find work, but without success, because of her awkward last name. But there was another Maria Concetta who she had almost stopped making herself heard: my fiancée.

In December 2004 came the sentence of the first instance which sentenced me to fourteen years and six months, and this gave a decisive shock to her choice of life. While I was living waiting for a return, Mari wrote me a melancholy letter but decided: "I can't stand this situation", "Loneliness is heavy", "Not that I can stay to wait all my life at Corleone", "The penalty could even increase", "I do it especially for my sanity", "I'm sorry", and another series of more or less plausible justifications. It seemed that she was the only one who suffered, while I had chosen to take a vacation. To the initial understanding and sympathy, a shot of pride took over, of which I needed it for many reasons. Dear Mari – I replied – I read your letter and I understand what you say but I do not justify it. It is not right to address these words to me precisely at the worst time of my life, when instead I would need you. You go away and I will not hold you back. But know one thing well: I will come out of here soon - earlier than you read in the newspapers. I will go out and I will come to Corleone, and then it will be too late to think again. Your choice, you did it, and I wish you all the best. But for me you will never be able to return. From that day I found an extra strength and the facts proved me right. When I came back to Corleone, four years later, I saw Maria Concetta again. I greeted her and passed by, without anything to add. That letter had closed the love story, until then, the most important of my life. Ten years begun with that stolen kiss in the abandoned villa of Pappalardo and ended up here, in the prison by Sulmona, with a few words on a piece of paper immediately shredded. I looked out the window of my cell and I went back to breathing.

Chapter 22: Addio, appuntato
Goodbye, appuntato

For some technical errors too much time had passed since it had been expressed the judgment of the second instance with respect to the final judgment of the Supreme Court, which was late to arrive. So, in 2007, the lawyer said there was a vague possibility of me getting out of prison even without having completely finished my sentence. I may be able to wait for the final sentence as a free man. I obviously pretended not to believe it, but I had already begun to daydream about my homecoming.

It had been five years since they had moved me to Sulmona, and I had taken the right measures to survive here. The other detainees and I knew each other well by now, and that phenomenon had been established for which the prisoners become a second family with which to share anger and pains, but also a lot of laughter. The day set for the hearing was the 27th February 2008, but in prison I did not get any good news.

"So, Salvatore, do you go out or not?" they asked me all the next morning, during the hour free in the gym. By now the restrictive measures they had changed, and I could go to the common areas to socialize, as well as having a small tv in the cell.
"No. The hearing was yesterday. Had it gone well they would have freed me by midnight."

"So, what now?"
"Now I have to do at least another three years here. Then we see."

"Except, do you know that tonight I dreamed of you?" said Franco, a Calabrian prisoner with which we had become good friends. "I have dreamed that they set you free! Minchia what a beauty!" "I wish, Franco! I know I'll keep you company for quite a while, however."

While I was still finishing speaking, a guard approached our small group.

"Boss, what are you doing, taking a couple of weights too?" I joked. "Do come little witty, Riina. You go to the registry office." "Mutherfucker!" exploded Franco, "The registration office! They are letting you go, Salvo!" All excited, I followed the officer, ready for the great news, but, to my sad regret, it was only a sheet that was submitted relating to permits for phone calls. As usual, administration contributed to increasing disappointment. I explained everything to the others, then went back to the cell.

When it was lunchtime, out of habit, I always turned on the television to follow Studio Sport and listen to the latest news on the Series A. But that day, who knows why, the TV was on Rai1. It was the thirteen, the time of the news, and I was in front of the sink to rinse my face, little interested in everything else. Suddenly from that I was distracted, the news became overbearingly loud in my ears. "... and it is a few hours ago the news that "Salvo" Riina, second son of the super boss Totò Riina, will be released for effect of the terms. Salvatore Giuseppe, detainee in Sulmona prison since 2002 by association mafia, was convicted in second degree..."The news continued but I had already stopped hearing. I looked over and saw my photograph on the TV. It was all true; they were talking about me! From the other cells began to arrive cries of jubilation.

"Salvo'! Have you heard the television?"
"To Tg1", shouted another,
"They said that you are free!"
"Hooray Salvo!" they shouted with an extraordinary participation. I was stunned, still no one had said any of this to me. I called the officer to ask permission to shower. As I walked down the aisle to reach the showers, the others looked out, they called me, gave advice and encouragement. I just thanked them, hoping that for once a journalist had brought me accurate good news. In the shower I was elated, I thought about what I would do as soon as I was free, who would I go find first, what I would eat once at home. It would be nice to hug my mother again.

When I returned to my cell I didn't have to wait long before they came. They brought empty bags to be filled with personal belongings, as it was done at every transfer. "Riina, there you go." He seemed to be smiling too. "Put what you want to bring. Hurry up that the appuntato is coming." "That horns of the appuntato?" I laugh. They all called him that, "the cuckold ".".

In prison there were guards that were helpful and understanding, but other characters they were as unbearable for us as they were for their colleagues. Once, to walk just a short stretch of corridor, they had forced me to keep handcuffs on my wrists just for the sake of humiliation. To which I replied.
"Cuckold, you can keep me the handcuffs as much as you want, but remember that from here I have to go out", indicating the front door section.
"We'll see," he replied. Finally, that cuckold of the constable came and spoke the three words I dreamed of for years.
"Riina, you are released from prison. I will remind you, that

you must first empty the cell", he added with resentment. "I'll take what I need.". The rest I will give or throw it away. Did he see that I was right now? I told him I was going to get out of that door. I smiled with taste of winning in my mouth.

At the prisons' registration office they told me that I would have to go immediately to Palermo to fill out some other cards. Then I went down to finish filling my inseparable red bag. I put on a white jacket and was escorted by two agents as I continued the walk to the main gate.

"Riina, it is from this morning that there is not a moment of truce", one of them told me.
"In what sense?"
"The phone just rings. Dozens of journalists who want news about him and about when we let him out." "I missed the journalists", he said. "But I'll need a taxi." "No use," explained the other. There is a black car waiting for him out here." "A black car?" My heart swelled a little more. "It's his family. They are waiting for him." The five-meter-high gray gate opened wide in front of me and the cops accompanied me for another ten steps. I saw not far away a parked Mercedes and the door behind open: there was my sister Lucia standing staring at me with a wide smile. We embrace, happy, with her and with my mother, with the same strength that we had put in June six years ago. Those few journalists were of no use who had made time to get on the place with cameras and microphones wanted news, and I replied by putting my bag in the trunk of the car and finally going down the road. During the trip we talked all the time. I told the details of that day, we laughed like a family coming back to breathe. With my eyes I watched it flow that landscape that I had learned by heart from my cell window. It was the same that I had also seen in

my trip outward. But this time, on my head, there was no longer any bar.

Chapter 23: Lucia si sposa
Lucia gets married

The joy of my early and unexpected return gave me a chance to reflect on my future and above all to stay with my new family. July 23rd, 2008 would be my sister's Lucia's wedding, and my presence I saw as a small miracle that I had been granted.

The judge, pending the judgment of the Supreme Court, had given me three years of special surveillance to be followed by two more years of probation. The special surveillance was limiting, but finding myself in Corleone it already seemed a lot to me. I had the obligation of three signatures per week, the ban on exceeding municipal boundaries and daylight hours within the which ones to be able to move – from eight in the morning to eight o'clock in the evening. It was a day of celebration that even journalists and the curious, who we were staring at polemics, failed to ruin. Vincenzo, my future brother-in-law and I, we went on to have a good time. Going from the barbershop, then to the bar for one last coffee on Wednesday morning, Corleone was sultry and torrid like every summer and, through my inseparable Sunglasses, I stared at every detail to make sure everything was okay. "Riina, a picture! Riina, an interview!" they shouted with a microphone in hand in front of the church of Maria Santissima dell'Immacolata. Many cameras stole images of our expressions of disappointment, to transform them then, in the news, into defiant looks.

"Look, you have to give us the copyrights as author then!", I tried to joke, turned to a camera. But I felt agitated, less serene. What tourists had to do with a moment of normality with my family, I cannot understand. One cameraman pushed another spectator, and a viewer yanked a journalist who was huddled against an invitee: oppressed as inside a football stadium. A couple took pictures with the smartphones, other curious people felt inside of an American film. Finally, we entered, closing in a circle of applause for my sister who was brighter than usual. It was the mirror of happiness. She greeted everyone, even the cameras, as I let the veil go down on her face, before the walk to the altar. Just sitting, she held hands with Vincenzo, caressing her through a white lace glove that my mother had chosen to wear for that day.

In the church were a hundred guests, surrounded by a decoration of white roses in vases in every corner. Don Giuseppe, from the altar, spoke and explained the responsibilities of love. At the moment of the blessing Lucy and Vincenzo came out of their kneelings and off they went with paper in hand.

An unscheduled reading for us invited, and for the objectives that from afar resumed the scene. "We want to thank the Lord for the blessing received on this day. Thank you to all those who have been close to us in these years", read Vincenzo. "And our thoughts also goes to those who are not here today. Salvatore, Gianni, Leoluca, we miss you. You have been here with us and you have given us peace and serenity." Journalists took notes, while I was moved.

We were a family changed, grown and always united, and my brother and my father could never again attend a party like this. Only at the reception, again, we were allowed to complete the feast without eyes prying eyes. We were all there: my uncle Gaetano, Aunt Giuseppa, my sister Maria Concetta with Toni and little Marilù to act as a bridesmaid. My mother joked and smiled, she even seemed actually happy. Inside she had everything, with her elegant appearance and discreet, dignified and safe, I saw the suffering she felt at the thought of those who wasn't there.

"What are you doing here, let us enjoy a party, for once. If you want more information you can ask the lawyer" she had resentfully replied to a journalist, first still to enter the church. She knew that at any moment I could be lost again, just pronounced the final judgment of the Supreme Court, and she wanted to preserve the best memories of that day. The second arrest also took place at night, accompanied this time by a spectacularization major by not-the police, but the Carabinieri. No need to choose a moment so unpleasant to validate an order that already waited, yet the door of house shook another time, making us jump from the bed. The military had invaded alley Scorsone with their cars, and everyone was wearing hoods blacks so as not to be recognized. Machine gun in his arms and bib with the inscription "carabinieri" in nice view: it looked quite like a scene from a skit. And in fact, behind them, there was no lack of official camera, which told my exit of the house and the looks of the aunts. That video would have gone around the world. I had the serene face, albeit estranged from sleep.

"Colonel," I said to the commander,

"does it seem like the way to make this brothel?"

"What brothel?" "Look here! All this show for one arrest? You also have recovery."

"What do you expect" he stated, "here too the show must have its part."

"But for what, it is definitely not a raid!"

So, I followed the parade of men in balaclavas and I mounted on board one of the police vehicles. Then they finally turned off the lights of the camera. So on January 9, 2009, I passed one more time to the Ucciardone prison, five days of detention pending the verdict of the President: eight years and ten months. subtrahend the penalty served in Sulmona, remained another two years, to be served this time in the district house of Padua.

In April 2009 the collaborator of justice on duty he pulled out new sensational revelations. This time, according to the confidences, it was said that from inside the prison of Padua I had exchanged information with other detainees, planning, among other things, an attack to Minister Alfano. The Public Prosecutor's Office of Catania, and not only that, he had serious doubts about the reliability of these statements, but still I prepared for a new transfer. It was the same story I had been living since 1993, just arrived in Corleone. A kind of ostracism for which anyone speaks, if he speaks negatively of the Riina family, he must certainly be right. I had only five months left of detention, and this time the chosen prison was that of Voghera.

The transfer took place according to the procedure already accustomed to, but the stay was different from those experienced so far. In the cell I had a comrade, Antonio, and we joked often. He had been there for many months, and he explained to me all the facilities, detention rooms, places and habits. He was fixated with the theater, and so he did part of the prison company. Antonio was also detained for associative crimes, he would be released ten days earlier than me. Fatalist like my father, I liked his way of always looking ahead, counting the days that remained. "A chiagne 'u murte sonde lacreme pérze " he told me. He who mourns a dead man wastes their own tears. It was with this wickedness that we had to get by.

Chapter 24: Un ergastolo in bianco
A blank life sentence

I spent my last five months of prison remembering everything about my life. My childhood, family, fugitive and the arrests, Corleone and my adventures, the last phone call to my dad from here, from the prison of Voghera. He had asked me how I was, and at that point he was rather sick. Since 2003 he has been hospitalized several times for heart problems, had undergone operations and a pacemaker, but the Supreme Court wanted him still isolated at a maxium penitentiary, without granting him anything, not even in the face of illness. Likely I wouldn't see my father again, so I try to hold tight all our photos and his words. I will never share the penalty that was inflicted on him, as well as on my brother and to me. We are "Not obliged to share, but only to respect. I returned a free man the day October 1, 2011, and immediately I was sent in Palermo and then in Corleone. I dodged many journalists thanks to a quibble that allowed me to go out a day before what everyone expected, so this time those who were disappointed were them.

No camera immortalized my clothing, my face and company who welcomed me. For once I had the sweet feeling that the world had forgotten Giuseppe Salvatore.

Corleone today has a new mayor who says he doesn't want me, just as I don't want Corleone. Not now. I asked to go away from there, because six months of special surveillance already made me understand that I was always at risk. It was enough for me to talk to someone to be accused of doing business with suspects, it was enough for me to respond in tone to a cop to be labeled as a man dangerous for the community.

My father and mother were born in Corleone, and I love this city. But already from Voghera I asked my lawyer to serve what I have left in Padua. In jail an expression is used: "life imprisonment in white", and it was what I risked if I stayed in Sicily. A continuous search for excuses and pretexts by the authorities to make me compromise: places, friendships, people. A way to extend the piece by piece surveillance until I don't get out of it anymore and make me return to jail. A blank life sentence.

In Padua, on the other hand, I have everything. Registration at the university, the first months of work in the association Paduan Families Against Marginalization and Drugs, opportunities of work in Vicenza.

Twenty-six months of special surveillance left, only six of which I spent in Corleone, before fleeing to the north. But it's never enough, and in Padua I also live other years of sacrifices, probation.

Probation gives larger spaces than to special surveillance: it is a penalty accessory that imposes on me the obligation of only one signature per week, the prohibition to go over the provincial territory – and no longer municipal – and the usual curfew every night. I can also ask for special permissions for parties, and so come back sometimes to visit my mother and sisters. I always sign, stage by stage, every move made from the Veneto to Sicily.

When I asked to come to Padua, and then when I was able to move, they began to talk about me even the local newspapers, and especially politicians. In the wake of the election campaigns, I heard about in the news and on talk shows regional presidents, presidents of the province, mayors. The name of the Riina is often only useful for advertising. In

2011 the Lega Nord worked to install about twenty banquets around the city, looking for signatures for my oust from Padua. Yet I continued to walk around the city and to see those tables without anyone recognizing my face and really cared about it.

I am with extraordinary people, the Venetians, willing to welcome everyone as long as you pay your own debt to justice. And then there is someone more distracted.

"Good evening sir, do you want to sign?" said a twenty-year-old boy with a local accent.
"What is this all about?"
"Against the presence of Riina's son to Padua. It is our job to send him away from here!"
"Ah, really? And why?" I insisted, trying to hide my cadence.
"How why? Because here we do not want these people related to crime to contaminate our city."
"Padua as a new Corleone, in short."
"That's right, you understand the problem! If you want, you can sign here."
"Later", I smiled, "because now I am in late.'

They hoped to collect at least a thousand signatures, and instead the leaguers collected less by a third. Even less than those who had enrolled.. Who launched this campaign against my name he won his elections, and that was enough for him to no longer need of slogans against the South. But Padova is also the city of culture, of young people, arcades and walks. A place where I learned to regenerate and to move freely, on foot of course, given that the driving licence is not granted to me, occasionally I would ride with the bicycle, being careful of theft, and I try to forget that the boundaries of this province are the boundaries of my freedom.

With the policemen we say "Hi" on the street, if I recognize them and they recognize me, and it's rare to find someone who wants to raise your voice, because where there is respect, there is no more is needed. I don't know yet how long it will take, but here at Padua I will take back my life.

Chapter 25: Diritti e doveri
Rights and obligations

I began my ordeal of trials and detentions on June 5, 2002, and I believe that this the journey will never completely end.

"Rest assured, Salvo," my father told me. "Chiù scuru i menzanuotte un pò fari" The darkness of my life was interspersed from small flashes of light that encouraged me to move forward: the marriages of my sisters above all. My brother's darkness Giovanni, who is just a year older than me, it will last a lifetime. And this is a pain constant that will cross my thoughts also when I feel like I'm happy, even when people will have forgotten about my surname.

I found love in Padua, I found friends to have fun with, I learned not to read the stories of the newspapers that they talk about social parties, designer clothes, sun glasses and luxury cars that I cannot even drive.

The testimony of my life has shown that I am used to All. I was given a penalty that, innocent or guilty, served with great dignity. I did not back down in the face of the State and I let the court speak.

The laws are always respected: the serious ones, the absurd ones, the foolish ones that can seem wrong. I will respect them all, even those that for my conscience are unjust. And I will also pay where my heart knows to be innocent.

What I have become I owe to my parents who did not miss me nothing and this is the answer I will give to anyone who wonders about the mafia seen on television. The happiness of my childhood, when I looked at Milan sitting in an armchair with my father, when we cooked together, when he scolded Giovanni if he made me spite: this was us, outside of all.

Maria Concetta who told fairy tales goodnight to Lucia, she who passed by the hours to color everything with markers, my father who read and repeated stories to us of Sicily, my mother who taught us the names of relatives in the photos. Everything else that belonged to us and will never be soiled by no insult and no trial.

It is since January 1993 that I have not been able to hug my father, and neither have my sisters and my mother. I think of him in a hard isolation that never anyone else has ever suffered, victim of a public and political anger that does not know and maybe he will never understand what I have instead saw.

From that January 15th I started my second life, and now I'm ready for a new jump, because there is always a need to fight, with speech and with memories. This book is my way to start over and tell who my family is. Every being has the right and duty to love their parents, and I will keep forever faith in this commitment.

> I am not the son of the "chief of chiefs". I am the son of Salvatore "Totò" Riina.

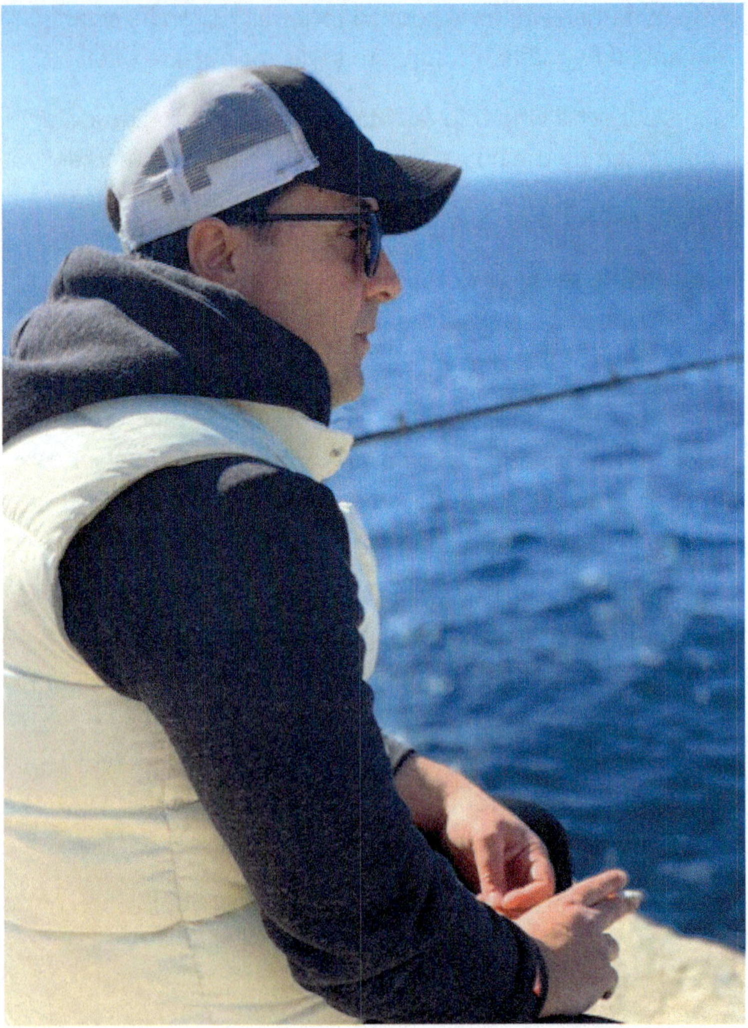